THE CINEMA OF
PAOLO AND VITTORIO
TAVIANI

Lorenzo Cuccu

THE CINEMA OF
PAOLO AND VITTORIO
TAVIANI

Nature, Culture and History
Revealed by Two Tuscan Masters

GREMESE

Cinema Series
Books of cinema for schools and universities

Acknowledgments of the author:
The author would like to thank: the Centro Cinema Paolo and Vittorio Taviani (particularly the President, Maria Fancelli), the Municipality of San Miniato, the Province of Pisa, the Tuscan Region, the Museum of Modern Art and Cinecittà Holding that promoted the publication of this volume; Antonio Monda for his friendly cooperation and for acting as a precious go-between with the Director of the MOMA, Lawrence Kardish and his collaborators; Mrs Franca Giani of the Municipality of San Miniato, for her help in the relations with the local administrations; Mrs Gianna Bernardini of the Filmtre of Roma for her cooperation in the research of the photographic material and for the suggestions on films; the translators Ilaria Fusina and Meg Shore for the brilliant result of their difficult work; Cristiano Giometti who translated the captions and editorial texts with great competence and generosity; my friend and collaborator Maurizio Ambrosini for his intelligent collaboration in the selection of the material for the iconographic section of this volume; Lucia Cardone, for her sensitive and qualified collaboration in the selection of the iconographic material and for the realization of this book; the other authors (Sandro Bernardi, Stefano Socci, Lucia Cardone), for the high quality of their essays and Guido Fink for the authoritative introductory note; and especially Vittorio and Paolo Taviani for their generous availability and for the conversations that enriched my work and deeply improved my knowledge of their films.

Photographic credits:
The shots are by Umberto Montiroli. The shots come from the archives of the Author, of the Laboratorio Cavalieri of Roma, of the Centro Cinema Paolo and Vittorio Taviani of San Miniato (Pisa) and of the production company Filmtre of Roma.
As far as possible the Publisher has tried to find the names of the photographers whose photographs are published in this volume, in order to attribute them correctly. However, this research has not always been successful and therefore the Publisher apologizes for any possible errors or omissions. In the event of reprinting the Publisher declares himself ready to make any necessary corrections and to recognize any rights, according to article 70, from law number 633, 1941.

Cover photos:
Scenes from *Elective Affinities* (cover) and *Good Morning Babylon* (back cover)

Original title:
Il cinema di Paolo e Vittorio Taviani – Natura, Cultura, Storia nei film dei due registi toscani

Translation from Italian:
Meg Shore, Ilaria Fusina, Cristiano Giometti

Graphic Design and Phototypeset:
Graphic Art 6 s.r.l. – Rome

Printed and bound by:
centro poligrafico romano – Tivoli

Copyright GREMESE
2001 © E.G.E. s.r.l. – Rome

ISBN 88-7301-466-6

CONTENTS

Giuliani De Negri,
between the two
directors. He was their
first producer, but also
the friend and the
elder brother who
protects and leads.

FOREWORD

BY GUIDO FINK

Nearly forty years have passed since, in an afternoon screening at the Venice Film Festival, a work by three directors making their debut exploded on the screen with totally unprecedented intellectual and expressive power. Interpreted by a young actor from the theater who had appeared only two or three times in small movie roles, the film involved us in infinite discussions that willingly shifted from the field of esthetics to that of political and ideological debate, and back. I am referring, of course, to A Man for Burning, directed, as they then said, by the "Taviani-Orsini collective," and acted by the extraordinary Gian Maria Volonté. I too was at that screening, as a rather peripheral part of an inured team of critics, centered around the magazine Cinema Nuovo and the beloved and feared father-figure, Guido Aristarco. Our group immediately began to champion this film, which was so powerful, so young, so capable of disturbing and provoking, and we were ready to defend it, with all our acerbic dialectic, against our colleagues and rivals. We then discovered, with surprise, that the film had also won over the enemy camp, those connected to the magazine Filmcritica, which, compared to our journal, were more aligned with estheticizing and modeled on positions arriving from across the Alps. And barely three years have passed since the memorable evening in San Miniato (the marvelous Tuscan town where Paolo and Vittorio—unfortunately no longer working with Orsini or Volonté—were born and raised), when the directors showed a splendidly restored copy of their first memorable film, "adopted" from their town, and still intact in its freshness and its generous and disruptive "newness."

In all that time, whether we realize it or not, the cinema of the Tavianis had always been with us and alongside us—in the violent ruptures and fervid hopes of the Sixties, as amid the dark years of terrorism and strategies of tension of the Seventies, captured in a recently published book by Marco Belpoliti, where he reconstructs the echoes and counter-coups of that period, recorded by writers such as Pasolini, Sciascia, Calvino, Fortini, Eco, and Levi. And the Tavianis are with us still, in the rapid and often unexpected upheavals, in a country and a world that is undergoing increasingly rapid and global transformation. With us and for us, they have confronted all the crucial themes of a country that finally emerged from immobility and faced the urgencies of change: the battle for divorce (Marriage Outlaws), the end of the Old Left and the confused entreaties of the world of young people (Subversives, Under the Sign of Scorpion), the solitude of the unarmed prophet (St. Michael had a Rooster), the seductions of the return to order and tradition (Allonsanfan), the insurmountable wall that still divides the marginal areas of the country from modernity (Padre Padrone). Then there was a need for renewal, to rediscover virginity, in touch with the world of nature and fable (The Meadow), which allowed them to re-evoke, in the language of legend, the most dramatic pages from the past (The Night of the Shooting Stars), or to rediscover a new energy through the eternal youth of cinema (Good Morning Babylon). And finally there has been direct and mature confrontation, never merely illustrative or passive, with the masters who have always guided them as an implicit model: Pirandello, Tolstoy, and Goethe.

But what is striking today, reviewing the Taviani's cinema, is not merely the urgency and relevance of the crucial themes that they have known how to face for us and with us, through films that are sometimes very beautiful and sometimes (as it happens) less resolved. It is the power of their very presence, as authors and prime viewers within the picture, which is then modified, faceted, made more complex. From the first shots of A Man for Burning, the most careful critics pointed out that what we were seeing on the screen was part objective, realistic in nature; and part completely subjective, fantastic, the fruit of Salvatore-Volonté's feverish imagination. But this wasn't all. The critical and searching glance of the films' authors was evident, palpable, watchful, and ever-present. They absolutely refused to allow things and persons in their shots to remain neutral, tranquil, or undisturbed. There is a type of cinema, widespread especially now, that avoids involving us, that shows us bodies, faces, backgrounds, and settings in merely two-dimensional fashion, restful and tranquilizing. This is just cinema, purely and pleasantly cinema. What the Tavianis do—which can make us debate and even anger us—is adamantly cinema of another sort.

Guido Fink

LORENZO CUCCU

NATURE, CULTURE AND HISTORY IN THE FILMS OF PAOLO AND VITTORIO TAVIANI

The work of Paolo and Vittorio Taviani is clearly among the most significant contributions to Italian postwar cinema, on both a cultural and an artistic level. It is characterized by a depth and seriousness of discourse, by the expressive power of the images and stories, and by their ability to link a search for an original language with a transformation of literary, figurative and musical traditions into a vivid tool of expression and awareness.

We will follow the chronological development of their oeuvre as one might review a journey— revisiting their various phases of study, with a progressive revelation of the works' profound essence and a purification of themes and forms.

And we will attempt to understand the structural constants in this body of work, where form and content are concentrated and oscillate around two poles, one positive, or euphoric, and solar, the other negative, dysphoric, and nocturnal. From film to film, or from phase to phase, or within the same film and the same phase, these structural elements orient the authors' stance to the large themes they are addressing: political and ideological passions, first of all; then the relationship of man to nature, the source and origin of Beauty, and the tragic nature of existence; finally, the value of artistic representation within man's existential condition and history.

THE WAR AND THE FIFTIES: BACKGROUND AND APPRENTICESHIP

The two brothers were born in San Miniato (Vittorio in 1929, Paolo in 1931), a small Tuscan hill-town, and their adventure begins with their studies, first in Florence, then in Pisa, as the sons of a lawyer who wanted them to join the ranks of the professional class, but who also had instilled in them a taste for music, the arts, and literature.

Their childhood and adolescence in San Miniato was marked by the piercing experience of the war and this will become a memory that they will capture, as early as possible, in the imagery of their films—first in a "documentary," *San Miniato, July '44*, and then in *The Night of the Shooting Stars*.

In Florence, the May Music Festival fostered their fascination with music and sets, and the treasures of that city also taught them to see the landscape and faces of their region through the eyes of the great Tuscan painters.

In Pisa they became a leading force in the university film club, where they became familiar with the great tradition of auteur cinema and Neorealism, particularly the Rossellini of *Paisan*. As Valentino Orsini recalls: "… we first met, and this is no accident, in a movie theater, where we were watching a film (*Paisan*) and where there was a man, an accountant I believe, who was making a fuss because he didn't like the film. I knew the Taviani brothers somewhat, they knew

me a bit, but there had never been an opportunity for us to be in close touch…we reacted to this man with a certain violence, offered him money to go back outside, if he would only let us watch the film…"

This is a rather meaningful testimonial, because it allows us to understand both the "militant" manner in which, from the beginning, they have lived out their passion for cinema and the way this is interwoven with political or ideological passion. This will become one of the themes and moving principles of their artistic discourse.

The historical, political, and cultural setting in which these passions are rooted and take form, is one of rigid opposition between two different worlds that characterized the Fifties. In terms of international relationships, there was the cold war and a bipolarity considered perfect by some, but in reality already unsound and unbalanced, as history would later demonstrate. In terms of political relationships in Italy, there was the fallout from the elections of April 18, 1948, with a division of power among the constituent political forces and the allocation, more ideological than real, of distinct realms of social representation. The bourgeoisie and petite bourgeoisie was assigned to the Christian Democrat Party and its allies, and salaried workers to the Communist Party and the forces of the Popular Front. In reality the projection of international relationships on the Italian stage occurred amid the conflict between the forces of the government and those of the opposition, in the realms of both parliament and propaganda. But this did not take place within the realm of class struggle, where the "cycle of reconstruction" imposed its own laws, and the "duplicity of Togliatti and his followers, after the end of the phase of the "radicalization of the masses," begun in 1943, recognized the need for politics of social compromise and the simultaneous possibility of a strategy of affirmation of identity on an ideological and cultural level.

Vittorio's and Paolo's ideological and political education took place in a region where the memory of the Resistance, the struggle against the Germans and the Fascists, was particularly vivid and strong. And this was a historical phase during which a situation of substantial political and social compromise, which prevented any real attempt to overturn relationships of power, corresponded on the Left—almost like a sort of

compensation for the impossibility of acting—to a strong ideological radicalization. The "red passion"[1] of intellectuals and artists took shape within this context, which was blocked and yet charged with expectations that Utopia could be. realized. This conviction pushed artists to represent and envision that hoped-for state. Thus the "red passion" came to be identified with a "passion for self" and "self-awareness" that characterize a specific social and cultural figure, that of the "petite bourgeois intellectual." It was presented as a variant of a tradition that is Romantic and late-Romantic in origin, where the choice of the "irregular" social statute of an artist (of even more dubious reputation if we are dealing with a film director!) is experienced as a haughty and rebellious diversity, both in terms of the social class the artist comes from and its rules.

The representation of "red passion," which for the Taviani brothers is "Utopia," and the reflection on the furors and contradictions of the Hero that embodies it—on his fragility and inadequacy—will be the profound thematic core of their first series of films, those the critics have called their "political-poetic cycle" or their "Utopian cycle." But it is also true that this "red passion" is manifested in their work in a

[1] Remo Bodei, "Il rosso, il grigio: il colore delle moderne passioni politiche," in S. Vegetti Finzi (ed.), *Storia delle passioni*, Bari, Laterza, 1995.

thematic core of deeper and broader dimensions. This is why their films can be interpreted in the light of a precise hermeneutic hypothesis,[2] which sees the "passion for self" (the desire for self-affirmation and recognition) as the profound motive of the Subject of Modernity, as the factor of his creative action, making him a new Prometheus, the constructor of a new world. But this same passion can also be seen as the internal evil that lies at the origin of the Subject's decline, which turns him into a reincarnation of Narcissus, contemplating himself and his own passion. And if, according to this interpretation, the two figures have coexisted forever, it is also true that, as historical time has unfolded, the creative role of Prometheus has diminished while the figure of Narcissus has emerged ever more clear and dominant. In a period of decline, the bourgeois artist can use his work to represent this development, this final goal, in terms of lucid awareness of unknowing manifestation. Thus he comes to be a conveyer of a *false awareness*, which induces him to still think of himself as a Prometheus, and of the now merely narcissistic "passion for self" as Utopia, as a representation of the possibility of changing the world.

[2] I am referring to the complex and profound discourse developed by E. Pulcini in "La passione del moderno: l'amore di sé," in *Storia delle passioni*, in E. Pulcini, op.cit.

I will attempt to show that it is in this rooting of the historical destiny of "passion for self" that we find one of the aspects of the complexity of the Taviani's work. One of the elements of contradiction and movement lies in the oscillation between the illusory power of passion and the lucid awareness of its nature.

THE VOYAGE TO ROME. THE UTOPIA CYCLE AND ITS FRAGILITY. OTHER DISCOVERIES AND PERSPECTIVES.

Let us continue following the Taviani brothers along their voyage. After their apprenticeship (cultural work in the film club and at a university magazine, *Il Campano*), they directed some theater in Livorno and made some documentaries using a movie camera on loan from the Workers' Association. They decided to go to Rome, where it was possible to make films, and to change films in order to change the world.

They left with Valentino Orsini, having decided to work together, and this idea of cinema as collective work was a guiding idea, destined to become a method or a sort of trademark. From the start, it was the result of precise choices and convictions, as well as a

Sketch of a scene of *Fiorile* by Giuseppe Sbarra.

particularly intense way of experiencing their relationship as brothers. The idea of cinema as a collective work of art-gleaned, I believe form the writings of Vsevolod Pudovkin—fit neatly with their political convictions and, above all, linked the "making of cinema" to the tradition of the artisan's workshop. This continued to be a characteristic of the "Taviani collective," even after their separation from Orsini; this indissoluble fellowship gradually united the two brothers with producers Giuliani De Negri and Grazia Volpi, costume designer Lina Nerli, set designer Gianni Sbarra, editor Roberto Perpignani, director of photography Beppe Lanci, and composer Nicola Piovani.

Costume designed by Lina Nerli for Carlotta, one of the characters of *Elective Affinities*. The intense atmosphere of the film is often entrusted to the costumes.

But this voyage implies something else as well, which should be mentioned immediately. There are times when a voyage is something more than a move or a change of address: going to the city, as so much great fiction has taught us, is the inaugural act of a story, the beginning of the test to which the modern hero is subjected in order to demonstrate his virtue, to show himself worthy of taking on the conquest of the object of his desire. And so the voyage is a crucial moment in the acquisition of "competence," which in much great fiction, focuses more on the revelation of the Subject than on his behavior, coincides with the very content of the tale. In my opinion this is also true for many of the stories by the Taviani brothers and, in this sense, I think one can say that their departure for Rome assumes a symbolic value that is projected as a constant *topos* in their films.

Those who analyze fiction say that in narrative development the encounter of the Hero with a Space produces an exchange of values, those that the subject finds in the new space and those tied to the space from where he has come. Thus a conjunction is created between the two spaces, with a resulting axiological content that is dialectic rather than summary in nature. And so, if Rome is the space of testing and action, where one goes to "do combat in a certain direction," one goes there carrying and bearing within him the setting of San Miniato and the Tuscan landscape, the backdrop of tradition, memory, and basic values: the social and human environment, rich in types and figures and potential "stories" that will remain in one's memory, ready to re-emerge. There is also the visual environment, the landscape that stretches between Pisa and Florence, the landscape of farms and villas, parish churches and cathedrals, and the natural landscape, reshaped in vision and memory by the grand Tuscan pictorial tradition. This Space will be a constant presence, which will become imperative for the role it necessarily will play, going beyond pure background or pure figurative retrieval.

In Rome there were a few years of the usual apprenticeship, a meeting with the great Joris Ivens and, in any case, the confirmation that for them, documentary film (in this case, *Italy is not a Poor Country*, 1960), was only a "desire for cinema." Then, finally, in 1962 they made their first feature-length film, *A Man for Burning*, a project that was also the occasion of their decisive meeting with Giuliani De Negri.

Vittorio Taviani has said, "Today *A Man for Burning* looks to us like an act of love for Neorealism, for the aggressive period of the Resistance, for the birth of the workers' and peasant movement. At the time, we wrote that we were against the sentimental furors of neo-populism, against the consolations of political mythology, against the magical allegories of incommunicability, against the naturalism to which Italian cinema had been reduced in the late Fifties. As a first film, we thought about an autobiographical project, a character who was trying to understand reality. Our meeting with the figure of Salvatore Carnevale gave us the occasion to free ourselves from all the risks of an autobiographical approach."[3]

Certainly, the story of the Sicilian trade unionist—a historical and significant figure, represented in non-hagiographic fashion, charged with energy and civil passion and a contradictory narcissism that leads him to believe he is a messiah and to go astray in periods of paroxysmal crisis—reveals, in its narrative construction and formal layout, a desire on the part of the three Pisan authors to carve out an original and prominent position within the panorama of Italian cinema. It also reveals an "extremely personal concept of cinema…" that "…places the Taviani and Orsini within that international current known as 'new cinema', which was achieving its greatest results precisely in the early Seventies."[4] This was cinema that combined social and political themes with new linguistic research and which tended to revive in functional terms the freedom of writing of the *nouvelle vague*, of Godard in particular, and of the great Soviet tradition of montage. Here we see the first manifestations of formal themes and motifs: the strong feeling for landscape, the theatricality, but above all what Bruno Torri has pointed out: 'Salvatore is the first of the Taviani characters that belongs to a well-focussed typology, which will then recur in their cinema … the prototype of the 'extremist', the bearer of Utopia—the one who always wants to 'force the times', 'to get to the bottom of things', the man dominated by an *idée fixe* or, more precisely, by a revolutionary ideal, consecrated to defeat (to death), because he is too divergent, too much ahead of his time, but whose sacrifice still serves the cause for which he has been beaten."[5] The figure or role of the "extremist" is central to the

[3] The quotation is from R. Ferrucci (ed.), *La bottega Taviani*, Florence, La Casa Usher, 1987, p. 22.

[4] B. Torri, "Good Morning, Taviani, Itinerari nel cinema di Paolo e Vittorio Taviani", *Quaderni della bottega Taviani*, Pisa, p. 22.

[5] B. Torri, op.cit., p. 23.

Gian Maria Volonté is Salvatore in the first film by the Taviani brothers, *A Man for Burning*: this character was inspired by the Sicilian trade-unionist Salvatore Carnevale, killed by the mafia.

Facing page: The peasants, led by Salvatore, occupy the land.

Taviani's work, because of his nature, his dialectic, and his dynamics. He is central because he proves to be an updated version of that *Subject of Modernity*, characterized or obsessed by *amour propre*, by the love of self and the need for self-affirmation—which makes him a bit Prometheus and a bit Narcissus, as I referred to above. In other words, we should be clear that what is being presented and discussed, through the personality of the "extremist figure," is the Promethean and Narcissistic figure of bourgeois subjectivity in its declining phase, more than the subject of the revolutionary perspective, which is only a guise, if not an outright disguise. And what is truly significant is precisely the capacity for objectification, for staging the "red passion" and the "passion for self" as a "placing outside oneself and opposite oneself," to start a process of analysis that will also be one of self-analysis. It is also significant that, in the representation of this figure, there is the capacity to maintain a halo of "expressionist" subjectivity which can energize the discourse. In *A Man for Burning*, the process of examination and revelation occurs only at the beginning, but it is important that from the beginning the "red passion" is not only expressed, but also represented in its contradictory nature.

And so Salvatore, in *A Man for Burning*, is the first incarnation of the double nature of Prometheus and Narcissus that is hidden in the "red passion" and that is manifested, more precisely, in the ambiguity of a character that is at the same time a *projection* of the authors' ideology and the *object* of their analysis. These are the two poles between which the relationships of the Taviani with the figures they have imagined always oscillate. Thus, as we will have occasion to see, their attention to the impassioned Man and his "adequacy" becomes a generative constant element for the entire "political poetic" cycle of works, where the authors' "red passion" is projected into the staging of the Promethean Hero, and their lucid analysis is exercised, with increasing clarity, in his unmasking as Narcissus.

To summarize, *A Man for Burning*—with the debut of the figure of the "extremist" as the first incarnation of Prometheus/Narcissus, and with the capacity to immediately put forth the "problem of form," represents the antecedent facts of the position that the Taviani will come to assume in their "cinema of rebellion." This will represent one of the most vital tendencies in

Italian cinema of the Sixties. It is the paradigmatic and peculiar position of this approach that, more explicitly than others, attempts to join the participation in the "red passion" to a focus on the "question of art" (which, among other things, would cause the break with Valentino Orsini), but it also explains why the power and complexity of their deeper discourse will not be swallowed up in the failure of ideology.

After the attempt of *Marriage Outlaws* (1963)—which is interesting as testimony to their civil passion, but where the final result is uneven—there are two films that represent a new moment of confrontation with the explosions and contradictions of the "red passion": *Subversives* (1967) and *Under the Sign of Scorpion* (1969). These films are from an important phase in the history of the Italian Left and the ideological mutations of the "intellectual

A scene from *Marriage Outlaws*, five episodes and a prologue inspired by the Sansone law, the first timid project to introduce divorce in Italy.

petite bourgeoisie." In reality, the elapsed years were crucial for the transformation of Italian society, assailed by social tensions (the resumption of the workers' struggles which would reach their high point in the "hot autumn" of 1969; the clash between the reformist and "modernizing" needs of groups that were more engaged in international competition for private and state capital, in opposition to the conservative choices of more backward groups and the parasite classes) and political tensions (the divisions provoked by the passage from the centrist government formula to that of the center-left; the adjustment of the Italian Communist Party policies to the new conditions imposed by "peaceful coexistence," the polycentrism theorized by Togliatti in the so-called "Yalta Memorandum," and the death of Togliatti, with its great traumatic and symbolic impact).

After the blocked situation of the Fifties, there was a renewed dynamic in economic, social and political relationships, on both a national and international level, and the ideological stage became complex and contradictory. The "red passion" was torn: between loyalty and rupture; between defense of the "homeland of socialism,"

"polycentrism," and an emphasis on the third world; between reformist gradualism and the expectation of insurrectional rupture; between faith in the historical task of the proletariat and doubts introduced by theories of worker integration and the disappearance of classes; between the slow periods of "occupation of the ramparts" and tendencies toward "cultural revolution"; between the gray forms of everyday militancy and the seductive capacity of the forms of struggle that reclaim the "imagination of power"; between the respectability of the Third Internationalist morality and spaces given over to the explosion of the "personal" and the existential, glimpsed through encounters with youth movements.

It was now this ideological magma that was opened up to the "red passion," to the plan or desire for Utopia and its representation. This was the framework for the problematic tensions, tied to uncertainty of identity and perspective, that the Taviani assumed, and this was the climate into which they introduced *Subversives* in 1967. They explicitly took sides, declaring: "'It is necessary to make mistakes' could be the subtitle of our film. That is, not contemplation of the crisis—a stance that we reject instinctively

**An image from
Subversives.**

more than ideologically—but the awareness and rebellion of the crisis using less orthodox modes and tools."[6]

This desire to be aware of crises and the need to rebel against them, even making mistakes, is seen in the figures of the four Communist intellectual characters who are forced to face up to their own *inadequacy* by a grand mass event, Togliatti's funeral—a traumatic event and a crucial and pivotal point in the history of the Communist Party, but also an event of enormous emotional impact. One of these figures, Ermanno, is a young Tuscan photographer who has headed out to conquer Rome. He is egocentric and a bit megalomaniacal, and rancorously claims his independence from everything, family, friends, wife, and his comrades' civic-mindedness. Yet he maintains a parasitical relationship with all of them. Sebastiano is another figure, a drab official from a provincial party, who unexpectedly finds himself confronting the disturbing reality of his

[6] In *La bottega Taviani,* op. cit., p. 26.

wife's manifest homosexual tendency. Ludovico is another figure, a director whose political beliefs have become lukewarm. He seems to understand that his faith in the Promethean character of art, embodied by the character of Leonardo da Vinci in the film he is shooting, is wretchedly unmasked by his frightening reaction to the possibly incurable illness that has struck him. The last figure is Ettore, a militant in the Latin-American revolutionary movement. He has fled to Rome, revolutionary to the word, impatient with the tactical strategies of Togliatti and politically extreme ("I am reclaiming the truth of Utopia", "History doesn't happen it is invented...", "Long live the extremist.."). In reality he has grown somewhat soft from sex and Roman trattorias, and his militant rigidity vacillates before the dangers represented by a return to the political struggle in his homeland, where his movement has recalled him. For all these figures, Togliatti's funeral, the tension and emotion that runs tangibly through the "Communist populace" borne out by documentary images, and the awareness of

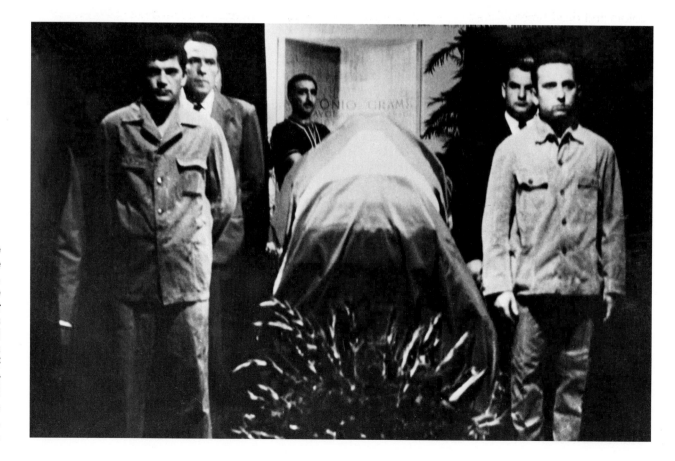

The activists of the PCI keep vigil at the corpse of Togliatti. In this film the depiction of a great mass event crosses with four individual stories, in which is analysed the rise of existentialist problems in the tired certainties of the ideology, the "red passion".

finding oneself faced with a fact of historical import that affects even their own existence ("Farewell Togliatti. Farewell to our youth.") function as a lashing reminder of the need to test their own adequacy and the need for a choice, a renewed commitment with their plans, their Utopia. Ettore's "ciao" at Togliatti's coffin seems to represent a confirmation of the desire to pursue Utopia, if not for all the characters, at least for the authors.

This renewed thrust of the "red passion"—polemical in terms of adaptation to the gray colors and dead times of a situation that seems stagnant only to those who wish to perceive it as such—and the reproposition of the "extremist" stance—now assumed more by the authors than by their characters—are ignited by a traumatic event, the "death of the father," which becomes the subject of a moving farewell, but also of a detachment. And this definitive detachment from the father accompanies a linguistic and stylistic detachment as well. The film makes a moving homage to Neorealism, represented here by the documentary shots of the funerals of the political father, but then insists on a search and examination of a "method" that confirms the original manner in which the authors are situated within the "linguistic revolution" of "new cinema."

And so the discourse on the necessity for Utopia and the work on form coincide, and this is a discovery. If it is a question of opposing the contemplation of crisis with the reasons for "red passion," two tools are needed. One is "understanding," that is, the choice of an effective cognitive strategy, which requires that the focus of attention shift directly to the forms and procedures of politics. The other is a suitable and renewed language of film. Thus, it seems necessary to construct, in exemplary and essential form, an opposition between the guiding idea of preservation and adaptation, and that of "utopian transformation." This is the opposition between the "gray passion"—the passion of those who are under the illusion that they can coexist with the earthquake that lurks beneath the surface of an apparently peaceful and in reality profoundly chaotic world (the chaos of the mode of capitalist production)—and the "red passion" of those who immediately want to attempt the risky leap toward the realm of Utopia, of Harmony in practice. Then, to be persuasive, to see that cinema contributes to

Under the Sign of Scorpion: a group of men belonging to the Scorpion clan spends the night on the beach.

changing the world, a choice is made to "personify" these guiding ideas into figures that have the representative power of mythological figures. And if the discourse is about persuasive logic, geometry, and strategies of struggle for power, if it is about modes of establishing and unmaking "parallelograms of forces," then this clash of opposing forces must seem to unfold within an abstract, extended space-time, cleansed of any trace of the contingent.

This is the discourse of *Under the Sign of Scorpion* (1968-69), the fable that tells of the mortal opposition between Renno and Rutolo, between one who has decided to coexist with the volcano and one who has decided, instead, to remove himself forever from its threat. This is a film that tells the story of the party of Power, torn between Utopia and Preservation. Behind the story, one can glimpse the tension between the two impulses that, at that time, were ripping apart the "Communist world" or, more correctly, its ideology. A group of men, only males, have escaped from a volcanic earthquake that has destroyed their island. They arrive on another island, also volcanic, inhabited by people who have learned to coexist with the volcano and

Renno (above)
and Rutolo (left), the
two chief characters
of the mortal struggle
between two
ideologies and
two strategies.

At the end of the battle the Scorpion clan won; they killed the men and raped the women. Among them there is also Aglaia, Renno's wife. A new conflict is going to start.

Renno is uncertain and asks a wise old islander's advice.

who hope they can predict and anticipate its moods. This is what the chief, Renno, says to Rutolo and Taleno, the leaders of the survivors from the Scorpion clan, who have decided to remove themselves forever from the threat of the volcano, to reach the mainland, and to construct a new society, free from the tyranny of nature's caprices. But to do so they need women, and therefore they must convince Renno and his people to follow them and to share their plan. Thus begins the competition for power between Utopia and Preservation, which unfolds according to the necessary movements of an algebraic equation. Utopia first tries the arm of Persuasion, of mimetic and emotional representation (from terrifying stories to a nocturnal and obsessive dance of men covered in sheepskins), to which Renno first responds with curiosity, and then, when the plan of the Scorpionites seems to succeed, with mournful fears alternating with vain affirmations of a sort of primogeniture of utopia. These mask the basic narcissism of power. But propaganda does not suffice; what matters is cunning and force, and the Scorpionites lose at this game and are imprisoned in a pit, destined to humiliation and death. But Renno, who represents the more doubtful and uncertain spirit of the Preservationist Power, commits a fatal error. He allows the Scorpionites to go free and live, but alone. Rutolo and his men then kill all the men on the island and abduct the women. However, once they reach the mainland they do not find Utopia, but History, that should have been finished and, instead, has barely begun: with the

battles between the sexes and social groups, the harsh conditions imposed by Nature; and the Rule of Necessity.

As one sees, the discourse of *Under the Sign of Scorpion* is one that re-fashions the inexorable logical development of mythological forms, with references to the Aeneid, to the rape of the Sabines, but also to Dante's Ulysses. This is a discourse that can speak clearly and have the public understand political symbologies. It is a discourse where the reflection on the "language of politics" and on the "language of cinema" meet. This becomes particularly penetrating when it turns into a reflection on the techniques of persuasion (the "provocations," the "terrifying tales," or the obsessive forms of gesturalism, and the resonance of the nocturnal dance) and it demonstrates an autonomous and functional ability to connect to linguistic revivals going on during that period.[7]

With this film, the discourse of the two brothers seems to believe adhere fully in to the "Promethean" function of cinema and art, in its possibility to keep alive the perspective of Utopia, meanwhile anticipating it in their representations, since the times still did not allow its concrete actualization. The "spirit of the

[7] Regarding these issues, see in particular L. Micciché's observations in *Cinema italiano: gli anni '60 e oltre*, Venice, Marsilio, 1995, pp. 248-149.

time" seemed to push them towards a cinema where representation is both comprehension and action. This cinema was a far cry from the staging of Subjectivity, with the contradictory nature of its passions and its disturbances that characterized the portraits of "extremists" in their earlier films, where one could glimpse the image of Narcissus that lay behind Prometheus.

In reality, Narcissus and his weakness are latent in the artist's pride, which believes in the possibility of getting energy from the Movement in progress, from its deceptive appearances, in order to anticipate the transformation of the world. Blinded by the Maja's veil of ideology and false self-awareness, one thus avoids the hard work of studying the real factors of what

Marx calls the "difficult question of times of revolution."

We shall see that the regression of a movement, which never was truly revolutionary, led the two brothers, along with Giulio Manieri and Fulvio Imbriani, to unmask Narcissus and the Deceiver that were hiding within the false Prometheus. But it also led them to take refuge and to renew themselves in the discovery of the happy and tragic possibility of representing the terrible Beauty and the inevitable Sorrow that lie in man's fate and in his relationship to Nature, Existence, and History.

In 1971, the Taviani decisively returned to the theme of competence and to a discourse that

St. Michael had a Rooster: the cruel *mise en scène* of the execution of the revolutionary Giulio Manieri.

The willingness and imagination of Giulio fight against the solitude and oppression of prison.

verifies the "virtue" of the figure that is presented as a "new Prometheus." *St. Michael had a Rooster* is the story of a failed revolutionary plan, a momentary victory of confabulatory fantasy, a mortal crisis produced by the confrontation with a world that has changed. Here one can transparently read references to a debate that had recently had an excruciating impact on the Left. The setting for the authors' discourse is again that of "red passion," but in reality the central theme is more profound. The introductory portion depicts Giulio Manieri who,

as a child, is punished and locked in a small room, where he overcomes his claustrophobia and fear of darkness, relying on the nursery rhyme in the film's title. We are made aware that, at the story's center, the Hero's virtue will be tested, in trials that Giulio Manierihimself feels called to face. Indeed these are the "tests of competence" represented by the deep semantic structure of the "formative fabric," the fabric within which the bourgeois hero typically puts himself to the test, during the phase of his ascent, as well as that of his decline.

There is a narrative path through which Giulio Manieriis put to the test—and through which he tests his own virtue as revolutionary head. He also tests the virtue of self-mastery, his ability to master his own anxieties. This is particularly significant in terms of his ability to semantically mobilize the space, or rather the three spaces that enter into the narrative dynamic: the space of the Umbrian countryside, so similar to that of San Miniato, where he doubts himself; the claustrophobic space of the cell, where he takes possession of himself and triumphs; and the space of the lagoon, the obsessive *Umwelt*, where he has a decisive confrontation and kills himself. This is the first true emergence of a semantically and structurally powerful role for the landscape, seen as an element of destiny and a source of mandate and sanction. The reference to the theme of competence and its semantic value becomes even more apparent if one thinks of the single viewpoint of the story. The cognitive horizon within which the viewer is located is always that of Giulio, with only two exceptions. One exception occurs when there is a debate about his fate and he is in his confined setting. The other occurs when the field splits, with the cruel introduction of a girl child,

sadistically suggesting a sort of "Griffith-like ending," but with the outcome reversed. Our hero must be killed, after all, and at the end, in order to represent the political dialectic that always remains in the film's thematic material, the camera "listens" to the reasons of the young militants, and also slightly explores their existence and pathetic contradictions. But the evaluative viewpoint—formulated on the level of values and affections—is Giulio's viewpoint, and it seems consistent with that of the authors.

There is a gap, a distance between the time of the action and the time of the narration, which by convention coincides with that of the viewer. The Taviani have abandoned the contemporaneity of their early films and have also moved beyond the choices of *Under the Sign of Scorpion*, where they constructed a temporal distance so broad and indeterminate that it could create a sort of "Primitive Scene." Here the gap is measured in such a way as to attribute a distance, and also a precise historical sense of reference, to the temporal scene in which Narcissus is emerging from the false Prometheus, from his attention to his own uncertainties.

Finally, the specific language of the images,

the way they are shot, offers confirmation. It is obvious, but also insufficient, to point out the frequency of the close-ups on Giulio. This becomes part of the single-perspective viewpoint of the tale and, throughout the central portion, is almost forced by the restricted nature of the space of the cell. It is insufficient because it is a monotonous choice of a type that would have reduced *St. Michael had a Rooster* to a "psychological" tale, which it is not. In terms of .

The attention on Giulio's face, in the prison cell and during the trip through the lagoon, shows the change of the authors towards an investigation of the frailty of Utopia and the Promethean hero.

During the encounter with the "new revolutionaries", Giulio feels incapable of understanding and to be understood. He becomes aware of his failure.

Right: The motionless and spectral lagoon seems to be the visual representation of Giulio's setback.

competence, the play of tensions between Subject and Object of desire—the value to be conquered, which in this case is his own virtue—and between the Subject and its Instigator and Judge, must be allowed to unfold. This happens when the Landscape is depicted as an exchange and tension with the Space. This leads to the role played by the extended surfaces of the finale: the wan lagoon, the cane thickets, and the spectral and distant city of Venice. But it also leads to the way Giulio Manieriis matched up with the camera shots, with the hills disappearing toward the horizon, with the view of San Jacopo, the village where he was called to prove himself in the initial part

of the film. The movement of the camera also plays a role, as a projection of the internal power of the character, capable of expanding the walls of his cell. And it also plays a role with the long, emotional combination of panoramic view and dolly shot that opens the finale. This is an illusory projection of power, if seen from Giulio's viewpoint, but also the introduction of the Figure of Defeat (the Space, the Landscape), if seen from the viewpoint of the Narrator.

Going back to the attempt to reconstruct the various periods of the Taviani's activity, in the development of a discourse and a coherent path, what is it that happens in the "movement" that traverses *St. Michael had a Rooster*? The theme of competence, the verification of virtue, is transformed into an issue of truth, the unmasking of Prometheus, as we have seen. But a new "guiding idea" began to open up in the story and in the ideas it produces: the idea of the power of the imagination and its ability to play an active role in man's existence and story. It is a guiding idea that we have already had to grasp as one of the skeins of the ball of yarn we must rewind, in order to reach the center of the labyrinth. And it turns out to be the new guiding idea that will lead, after Prometheus and Narcissus, to the discovery of Orpheus.

But there is one more step to be taken, which the authors achieve with *Allonsanfan* in 1974, three years after *St. Michael had a Rooster*. This step has been interpreted by many as a radical turn-around, or an about-face, from the ideological to the psychological, from "povero" or spare cinema to grand spectacle, from short-story with a message to great novel or melodrama.

The fundamental theme of the Disguise can already be seen emerging in perceptible fashion in the interweavings behind unexpected turns in plot. This permeates all elements of the film

Allonsanfan. Fulvio Imbriani (Marcello Mastroianni) shows himself to his siblings. This film marks the return to the melodrama as a formal and thematic source of inspiration.

Falsehearted Fulvio the traitor tries in vain to save his life.

Charlotte, his wife, is the first of the women deceived by Fulvio.

much more significantly than has been heretofore understood. The petit bourgeois Prometheus has reached the end of his explorations. In the dialectic of Being and Appearing, he has found the heart of the problem. In the figures and exchanges of the "semantics of Truth," he has found, beyond Narcissus, the archetypal figures of the Deceiver and the Betrayer.

These are figures that, in addition to being embodied in the principal character, are projected into the tightrope dynamic of intrigue, with its intersecting and echoing play of deceptions, lies, secrets, and disguises. These take on a fictional complexity, constructed from numerous points of perspective, and with a more intricately strategic regulation of the flow of information that is transmitted to the viewer. The figure of the Deceiver also has the function of giving profound meaning to the complex self-referentiality of the representation of the setting, explicitly evoked during the titles and skillfully orchestrated with all means of filmic representation. This is particularly true with the use of color, which can function introspectively projecting the emotions of the characters onto the external world. Or it can function dramatically and be spread over situations, to give them their basic tone. Or it can function strategically, giving the viewer advance warning of some turn in the narrative. This is also true with the music that is constructed on two fundamental themes. One has a euphoric and ironic value and relates to Fulvio Imbriani's push toward the "pink passion" of family life. The other, also subjective and euphoric, but also judgmental and ironic, relates to the "red passion" of revolution. In the arrangement of the music the repetition of two crucial moments becomes particularly effective.

The self-consciousness of the staging, which presents the figure of the Author as that of a grand Manipulator, duplicates the theme of Fiction that pervades the tale. It is precisely in this centrality of the theme of Being and Appearing that one can seek, and indeed find, the dynamic continuity of the discourse of the Taviani's cinema.

Allonsanfan represents the conclusion of a discourse and simultaneously, in the finale, in the "positive fiction" of the young revolutionary, revives a theme that we saw earlier in *St. Michael had a Rooster*. This is the theme of truth

The two scenes show the "rose passion" and the "red passion" that turn upside down the heart of the chief character. Both of them are associated with two precise musical themes, that of the "dirindindin" and that of the "saltarello".

and the active role of Fantasy, of the Fable seen as the positive solution of experience.

AFTER UTOPIA: CULTURE AS POSSIBLE DELIVERANCE; "HARSH NATURE" AND THE "COGNITION OF SORROW"

The path that led to the discovery of the inauthenticity of the petit bourgeois Prometheus has the disconsolate closure of the ironic discourse, in the sense that Northrop Frye assigns to this term. The discourse also remains happily open to new perspectives and, in the meantime, is made up of hypotheses of development based on acquisitions that will become its formal and semantic architecture.

We will now see that the Taviani's process of unmasking the Promethean ideology, through the analysis of the manifestation of the petite bourgeois intellectual's disguise as a false, uncertain, problematic, or conquered Prometheus, opens up two different ways of development.

The first is one that tends toward the representation of the radicality of the relationship between Man and Nature and the contradictory and devastating totality of the primary passions.

The second ends up overturning the value of the staging, which progresses from a formal reflection on the negative solution of the relationship between Being and Appearing to a positive manifestation of *marvelous representability*, in story and vision, of the events of existence and the history and appearance of the world.

As we know, both paths, the thematic and the formal, have been interpreted by many as being a defeat, an abandonment of the difficulties of cinema with a viewpoint, political cinema, for the empty glory of "auteur" cinema. This is seen as a surrender, on ideological terrain, through the passage from the "extremist hero" and the furors of "red passion" to the deceiving "gray-pink passion" of Fulvio Imbriani. It is also seen by some as a surrender on an artistic plane, in the passage from the experimentalism of "poetic political" cinema to the "magniloquent spectacle." Thus it is seen as a path of abandonment and defeat, with which the Taviani would passively accompany and endure the ebb tide of "revolutionary" hopes—first those of the postwar period; then those of 1968—in the gloom of the terrible the Seventies, the "years of lead," charged with inescapable violence and sorrow; and then in the passive quiet and progressive putrefaction of the Eighties.

In reality, this period of regression of workers' struggles and political and social compromise with which Italy responded in weak and contradictory fashion to the demands created by the crisis of the restructured global economy, the years of political terrorism with their murky national and international backdrop, seemed to no longer have room for Utopia. The Taviani brothers' abandonment of this theme, and of any direct or indirect references to possibilities of political and social transformation in the world, are both a result and a sign of this change. Nevertheless, I believe that one should interpret the path that the two brothers pursued from this time on, not in terms of "regression," but rather in terms of thematic and aesthetic examination. An inversion of sign was needed to evaluate the passage from "extremist" hero to "deceiver," a passage that, for me, is a process of unmasking the false awareness that is part of the profound nature of the false Prometheus. Fulvio Imbriani, the "deceiver," is not the opposite of Salvatore-Prometheus. He is the revelation of the profound narcissism that animates and motivates him, a revelation that is mediated by the figure of Giulio Manieri and his fragility. In this sense,

this process is one of maturation and examination, which in fact ties the Taviani's discourse to one on the narcissistic nature of the impassioned Hero. The latter thinks he is Prometheus only because he is impassioned, but who instead is only Narcissus, possessed and guided by an unproductive "passion for self."

It also should be said, apropos the process of formal and spectacular embellishment of the two brothers' films, that this is not a sign of surrender to academic beauty, but rather a way for their cultural and artistic biography to become the subject of problematic reflection, through the revival of a noble formal tradition.

As I have already mentioned, two ways, two possible lines of development arise at the conclusion of this path, this first part of their voyage.

The first is an acknowledgment of the existential and vital nature—the radicality, violence, and tragedy implicit in the relationship of man to nature, including the relationship man has within himself, with his primal passions and impulses. This is an ambiguous relationship, one that is contradictory and lacerating to the extent that it enters into conflict with Prometheus's "desire to exist," which clearly, despite it all, continues to be at work in the authors' universe of intentions and imagination. This is a line of discourse, of a theme already latent in the process of passage from the figure of the "extremist" to the figure of the "deceiver." Its effects will be seen in terms of the narrative model, with an increasingly pronounced shift from issues of competence to the typology of the ironic tale. And it will be seen in terms of recurrent iconography with the growing power of the presence of the landscape. Within this line of discourse, the landscape appears as an image of Harsh Nature, which challenges man to action (and thus assumes the role of Instigator) and remains unmoved by his failure or defeat (and thus assumes the role of the Judge who condemns him).

The second line of development is tied to the positive revival of the theme of Representation, of Staging, or Appearance. In the Taviani's earlier films, theatricality was a constant theme, tied to the themes of both narcissism and deception. There is the theatricality of Salvatore's behavior; it is a tool of persuasion and deception on the part of the Scorpionites; it is an illusory tool of survival and victorious struggle for Giulio Manieri; it plays a part

iconographically in the figure of the "deceiver" Fulvio Imbriani. But earlier, in the ending of *Allonsanfan*, it had appeared in reverse, in the affirmation of the positive value of Fiction, through the final dance evoked by the young Allonsanfon. And even within this line of development, the role of the landscape is reinforced, presented as a *Stage of Memory*, as a place of positive action, both source and repository of the grand Tuscan figurative tradition. To summarize and conclude, this is a line of development that turns Fiction, Representation, into a positive value, into a manifestation of the marvelous representability of the events of existence and the story, as well as of the world's "visibility." This is what BrunoTorri, like Cesare Cases before him, calls the conquest of the "spirit of the story," the power of the truth (including ethical and existential, as well as cognitive and artistic) of the Fable. I am speaking of the discovery of the active role that, within the narrative path that can be taken by Space, by Landscape, by the elegiac vision, attempts to recover the enchanted and voracious glances of adolescents. Or it can be a role played by the lyrical, contemplative vision, where Nature offers itself and its mysteries. This is the discovery of the importance of distancing the fable's temporal stage in the past, so that Memory can be granted the same role that the insistence of the glance assigns to Landscape. I am speaking of the discovery of Cinema as the Marvelous Stage and of its Creator as the Great Manipulator. These are the discoveries that will unfold fully in the "fable and enchanted vision cycle," which includes *The Night of the Shooting Stars*, *Kaos,* and *Good Morning Babylon.*

NATURE AS OPPRESSION, ORIGIN AND MANIFESTATION OF THE TRAGEDY OF EXISTENCE

Before we go on to the afore mentioned films, however, there are two more, *Padre Padrone* and *The Meadow*, which fall within the first of the two lines of development that I have outlined. This approach will then seem to be interrupted, only to reappear in the films of the Eighties.

The first of these two films, made in 1977, is taken from Gavino Ledda's autobiographical book, in which he tells the story of his liberation from the oppression of his patriarchal pastoral society. Here again the story addresses the "issue

of competence," but this time it is dealt with positively, no longer in the realm of political ideology, but in terms of the primordial values of harsh Nature and tyrannical Blood. The conquest of language is both tool and path for this process of liberation from the subhuman conditions of physical and mental isolation in which the young shepherd is forced to live, according to the rules of an archaic society, dominated by the rule of nature's necessities. First the protagonist conquers the language of music, which, with the sound of an old accordion, is projected over the landscape, almost transfiguring it. Music also becomes a tool for the communication and comprehension of emotions and ideas. Then Gavino conquers the Italian language and the languages of antiquity, which allows him to go on to conquer social relationships and friendship. Finally, he conquers literature, which allows him to dominate experience through its poetic representation.

This film also marks a change in direction in terms of the form of communication. The two brothers, aware of the need to reach a public broader than film-club supporters, choose television as their next means of communication.

The consequent need to "speak clearly" will return frequently as they continue along their path.

Critics who are too ready to accept innovation and too tied to the formula of "poetic political" cinema have tended to fault this film for its edifying optimism, out of line with the tragic irony of the Prometheus/Narcissus/Deceiver

discourse. But this impression can be proved wrong by the trembling that shakes the shoulders of the writer, a legacy of the ancestral worries that have marked him forever, a sign of the immanence of the tragedy in his existence.

Likewise, on the level of formal structure, the impression of giving in to the consumerist simplification induced by the work's destination

Padre padrone **introduces the theme of the cruel confrontation of human beings with nature and with the ties of social and cultural traditions.**

Music and art as a real
chance to be free.

The shepherd father hurting and threatening his son introduces
the figure of the tyrannical parent. The character of the blessing
parent will be opposed to this one.

for a television audience, in a language of film heretofore characterized by experimentation, is contradicted by a series of signals that one needs to know how to read.

First of all, from the point of view of structure, the tendency to emphasize the setting of the scene has not been completely abandoned. Here it reappears in the form of the prologue and epilogue, narrated in the first person by the writer, Gavino Ledda, who plays himself. At the beginning, shot at middle-distance against a white wall, he prunes a stick that he will give to Omero Antonutti is to who will play his father. He initiates the action with a sort of "indication of direction," that serves to point out the nature of the representation, the *mimesis*, in an Aristotelian sense, of the action that is about to begin. And at the end it is he, again, who concludes the story of his adventure and, as in popular stories, "draws the moral," comments, even raises doubts as to the full truth of his victory over the conditions of Nature and Tradition.

And then it isn't even completely true that it is he, the writer, who concludes the discourse. The last word is reserved for the Author who, in the guise of *Image-Maker*, holds his glance on the back of the writer and his insurmountable

trembling. It is through this framing of the story, through the construction of the tale's double level, that two effects are constructed. The first is an effect of alienation which, by lowering the level of referential illusion and secondary identification, minimizes the edifying function of the story. The second one seems to be telling us that, in the final analysis, the film is not the representation of the shepherd Gavino's story-with-a-happy-ending. Rather it is the representation of the uncertainties of Gavino Ledda, the man of letters, who is also responsible for the long tale that takes up almost the entire film. This is a textbook example of the non-coincidence and non-conformity of the Narrator personified by the Author. But, in this case, there is the sense of an additional intervention by the authors on the initial literary text, the sense of an interpretation that is also a vindication of the autonomy and dialectic continuity of the discourse itself.

The film has yet another dimension, which seems to escape or go beyond the boundaries of the discourse developed through Gavino's tale, of his more direct theme. This is the stance of astonished contemplation that the movie camera assumes vis-à-vis the world, its pure visibility and sound, the visual and sound landscape, an epiphany of Nature and its mystery. The narrative occasion is represented in particular by the episode of the first apprenticeship to which the father subjects the young Gavino, when he teaches him to understand the language of nature through noises. It is one of the film's highest moments from the point of view of expressive tension and, significantly, it is contradictory to and detached from the logic of the story. It is a sort of Orphism or ability to give shape to the unformed phenomenal flow, which the movie camera produces with its superior visual and auditory sensitivity. The camera can extract clear forms and sounds from the darkness and from the indistinct buzz, and immediately create images from them: the oak tree, the stream, true artistic epiphanies of the absoluteness of nature. And, over the course of the film, this amazement of the glance that is taking shape at other times is manifested through recurrent stylistic characteristics. This is accomplished through distanced framing, which absorbs the figures into the landscape, presented as an absolved and total presence, and through certain broad panoramas that at times assume a musical cadence.

In conclusion, if the film has the appearance of an edifying and consoling fable, expressed in language adapted to a television audience, its substance is a complex discourse. For the first time, the brothers' work addresses the theme of the terrible collision of man with the conditions of a society based on a brutal relationship with nature. But the discourse also opens the way to the representation of man's ability to free himself from these conditions through the tool of language and artistic imagination.

The Meadow was made in 1979, at the end of the difficult period of the Seventies. Here the authors used the tragic story of Giovanni, Eugenia, and Enzo to "express the sorrow we felt around us during these years," to represent, almost to exorcise, the death impulse that seemed to have struck an entire generation. It is a moment along their path and their reflection that, even more than *Padre Padrone,* seems completely contradictory in relation to the free unfolding of the pleasure of the tale and the vision that will appear in their next film. But we know that the artist's trajectory is never linear. It proceeds in spiral fashion and doesn't follow a straight line but, precisely like a novel, moves

Eugenia wounded by the indifference and violence of the adults. Giovanni's and Enzo's shadows seem to forecast the destiny of defeat and death looming over the three characters.

along interwoven paths with detours and apparent backward steps. And, just as in the novel, threads that seemed abandoned reappear at times or, to continue in the language of literary criticism, those threads that seemed like "satellites" abandoned along the road reappear unexpectedly as "cores," as essential elements of the narration and the discourse. In our case, what was the secondary branch that seemed abandoned? Was it the theme of the dialectic between the rationales of ideology and those of existence? This appeared so clearly in *Subversives*, and as a counter-melody in *St. Michael had a Rooster* or as the unmasking of the narcissism of the false Prometheus in *Allonsanfan*. But here it returns as the primary theme, proposing an inverted relationship between the two poles. There is an affirmation of the primacy of the rationales of existence upon which, however, the tragic shadow of the death impulse is projected, after the gray shadow of the urge to repudiate the red passion

The Meadow.
Giovanni, Enzo and
Eugenia (Isabella
Rossellini) on their
lawn, the place of
their tragic attempt
to build a Utopia
in sentimental and
social life.

of politics and Eros. *The Meadow* warns us, in other words, that behind the happiness of a path that moves from self-revelation to the discovery of the solar, invigorating character of artistic representation, there is the latent alternative of a tragic sense of existence. It warns us that, behind the splendor that the astonished glance absorbs from the landscape, hides the dark side that turns this same landscape into an instigator of death. One of the themes of the film, perhaps the principal one, is precisely that of the transformation that the landscape undergoes in the eyes of the protagonists.[8]

THE CYCLE OF THE FABLE AND THE ENCHANTED VISION

If in the films of the Seventies the first of the two lines of development, outlined above, prevail, the films of the Eighties are characterized by what Bruno Torri has called the cycle of the "spirit of the tale,"[9] which we might also define as the cycle" of the fable and the

[8] See Sandro Bernardi's essay in this volume.

[9] In *Good Morning, Taviani*, op. cit., p. 29.

The different way of feeling and looking at the landscape keeps pace with the inner transformation of the three characters.

enchanted vision." In these films the authors continue to stage man's tragic confrontation with the terrible power of nature and with the liberating but also devastating totality of primal passions. But they do so within a perspective where the happy, solar side of the worldview seems to dominate.

Three years after *The Meadow*, set in the Tuscan landscape of San Gimignano, they make *The Night of the Shooting Stars* (1982). It is another voyage of return, but of a different type, namely a return to the landscape of childhood and youth, to the tragic events that unfolded there, and to the distinctive memories that characterize it and transfigure it.

Here, the line of Memory that becomes Fable and Enchanted Vision is manifested, in an inversion of perspective from that of *The Meadow*. This change would be inexplicable if one didn't take into account the duplicity of perspectives that emerged from the first phase and the polarity of euphoria and dis-euphoria that unleashes the dynamics of the authors' discourse.

Certainly one also might see this film, with its quality of a popular epic, as a response, a counteroffensive of "political rationale" to the lacerating ambiguity and to the final death impulse where petit-bourgeois subjectivity has ended up. Certainly there is no doubt that the film also revives a political discourse, about the Resistance and a war that was also a civil war, as is now clear and accepted, and as the film openly shows.

But to limit ourselves to this perspective—and to reduce the polarities active in the Taviani's films to one between an "ideological" moment and "existential" moment—frankly, seems reductive and misleading. The way the eyes of Cecilia the child interpret the sorrowful and tragic material of historical memory, transfiguring it into events and mythological figures—revived by the voice/memory of the adult Cecilia character/narrator, who tells her child about those events as if she were reciting a fable, to put him to sleep—would make no sense. This is how the "battle in the wheat field" should be read, and not only in the moments when the transfiguration of the horror of the events in the Homeric image is linked explicitly to Cecilia and her imagination, nurtured by the tales of the peasant poet. This is how all the other episodes should be interpreted as well, constructed and connected according to a "logic of the

incomprehensible," a projection of Cecilia's dazed and yet fascinated and fantasticating glance.

This is also how we should interpret so many other moments that unfold under the sign of the "logic of marvelous transfiguration": the encounter of the two children with the American soldiers; the encounter with the "crazy man with the eggs." Even the scenes, terrible in and of themselves, where Galvano and his family listen to and interpret the roars that describe the explosion of their "red San Martino which has vanished," and the unexpected lights of the

shells that break through the blue of the night.

In other words, the significance of this transfiguring memory would be lost, a memory that extends its "tone" to all the events that the film represents, even to those that take place outside the cognitive horizon of the narrator/character. Some of these, strictly speaking, could be seen as "indirect memories," the result of later tales, stratified in Cecilia's memory. Others absolutely could not be: the long tracking shot, which is subjective, imaginary, and memorializing, where Rosanna reviews the important moments of her life in the

The Night of the Shooting Stars marks the beginning of a search for the "spirit of the tale". The story is indeed presented as a tale that a young mother tells to her child.

Three stages of the battle in the corn field: in Cecilia's mind the horror for the civil war is transfigured into the image of the wounded warrior.

now destroyed big house, the "vision" of the dying Sicilian, which must be attributed directly to the "Narrator of the first instance," to Gaudreault's *Mega-narrator*. And it is precisely the authors' choice of the latter, a choice, in substance, to adopt the "logic of transfiguration"—memorializing, fable-like, iconographic—that explains the particular type of delegated narrator proposed by the film. The reason lies in the choice to adopt a filter, a point of view, a tool of mediation, that is also anthropologically similar to that of the public to which the film is most directly and immediately addressed, and which thus represents an interpretive key to the film itself. It is as if the authors wanted all the viewers who see the film

These two pages: The adventure of Galvano and his companions develops with moments of horror and sensuality, of frightened and fraternal expectation, of a past love that returns.

to resemble the person represented by the delegated narrator, who is thus also the "model witness."

This interpretive key also is re-proposed through the direct activity of the narrating instance, immediately manifested, in that forward-moving dolly that projects its glance into the stage of memory, delimited by the window frame, at the very moment when the narrating voice begins its discourse. In this way it immediately becomes clear that the scene will be traversed by *two* glances: that of Cecilia, who recovers her childhood view, and that of the Author, who reworks the scene, especially figuratively. He does so with the technique of split and superimposed glances, which convey the activity and viewpoint of an *invisible spectator*, which is projected *today and from today* onto *yesterday's stage*, from the *present of the filming* to the *past of the represented action*: one example that can stand in for all the others is that long, intense panoramic left/right view over the landscape, which marks the transition from the terrible night of fires to the following morning, to the resumption of the walk of hope of Galvano and his followers. This is presented as subjective, but it isn't; instead, it is really the

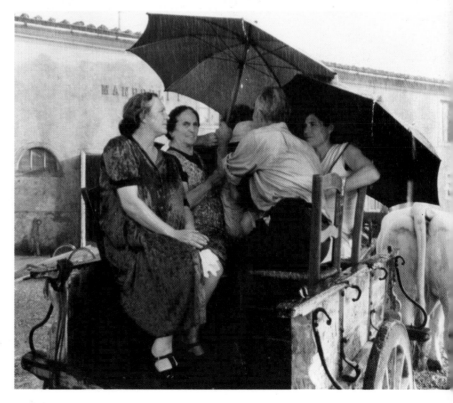

introduction of the "author's glance," which recovers and contemplates that scene, and it is as if it were being offered up once again to the action, to the passions, to the heart-felt view of the characters. This happens, again, with the technique of what I would call the "composition/glance"—the result of a complex elaboration that, in the Taviani's films, always passes through the preparatory work entrusted to set designer Gianni Sbarra, and to costume designer Lina Nerli. It also passes through the figurative memory that produces the "blocking" of the "action sequences" and the "attraction sequences" into "shot effects": suspensions of the linear flow into "iconographemes" that are not necessarily the result of precise pictorial quotations,[10] but where the figurative composition has the power of condensation, of symbolic configuration.

Through these formal choices, the authors, in *The Night of the Shooting Stars*, focus extraordinary attention on the representation of the landscape and the "figures in the landscape." It is an attention that passes through the mediation and re-composition of the landscape of memory of the narrator, with the landscape of biographical and pictorial

memory of the authors and then with the "rediscovered landscape" of the cinematographic glance in action.

Thus the complexity of this operation, carried out in the name of the "spirit of the tale," becomes clear. It likewise becomes clear how the task of conveying the Author's meditation—placed above the Author's subjectivity and the nature of his own memory—is entrusted to this formal complexity.

André Gardies has taught us that the Mega-narrator is also a "*partiteur;*" he intervenes in the construction of the film, even through the soundtrack, through the musical commentary, here entrusted substantially to three leading themes, or three different "tones," one elegiac, one epic, one dramatic. One should note, however, that if the camera work for the most part is aligned with the manifestation of authorial subjectivity, the music is aligned for the most part with the action represented, almost as if those musical themes were in some way taking part in the action. From a layman's perspective, I might even say that this use of musical commentary seems to derive from the experience of melodrama, neither internal nor totally external to the action, as Metz describes

---

[10] For the influence of the figurative tradition in the Taviani brothers' films, see I. Luperini, "The Tavianis' 'Tuscan Classicism': a Blend of Figurative Art and Cinema," in *Paolo and Vittorio Taviani. Poetry of Italian Landscape*, R. Ferrucci and P. Turini, ed., Rome, Gremese, 1995.

the voice of Orson Welles' *The Magnificent Ambersons.*

But there is a final "movement" in the film that must be considered, the one that marks its conclusion. This does not fade out into a return to the "scenic frame"—the mother and child in the large bed. Rather it is resolved with a slow backward tracking shot, whereby the Author's glance abandons this scene as well, as if it were also growing distant in memory. It is an inverse movement, similar but not identical in structural function, to the one at the beginning which moved from the frame to the scene of memory. I believe that this indicates that the memory structure of the film is "telescoped"; the story of the events of '44, told by the mother, is in its turn the "memory of a story." The act of memory thus is not only told in numerous voices—that of Cecilia, that of the Mega-narrator. It is also told in numerous stages, in numerous temporal segments. And so, in the end, the discourse tends to overturn onto its source and to place memory, but also the figure of the Author, at the center, in an accentuation of the problematically self-reflective nature of the discourse that the happiness of the tale and the glance must not hide.

Kaos (1984) is another voyage—prompted by a love for Pirandello[11]—this time directed southward, toward Sicily, toward a landscape that is Paolo and Vittorio Taviani's second landscape of choice. It is a primordial landscape, solar and yet charged with mystery. It is an apparition behind which one intuits the presence of ancestral forces: the image of the "realm of natural necessity," theater of a ferocious struggle for existence, traversed and struck by the violent and direct manifestation of primal passions, marked by the image of forces that are at the same time natural and supernatural: the moon which enchants and indelibly brands the child Batà; the nocturnal shadow that, passing over the threshing-floor, seems to produce the crack in the jar as if by witchcraft.

But it is also a landscape, in a universe where the poetic fantasy is generated and regenerated, captured in its Springtime state. It is a universe that rests on the boundary line between the world of nature and the world of culture, a "Viconian" scene where the "lumbering beast that is all senses," possessed by vital impulses, by carnality, by ferocity, begins to dominate through "fantasy" expressed in song, in gesture, in figuration, and in ritual.

[11] See Socci's essay in this volume.

natural and corporeal symbolism: the black cow ridden by the head of the brigands, rapists and assassins; the moon; the clenched fists beneath the mother's chin in *The Other Son*. Then there is another fist, belonging to Sidora, who strikes the back of her mother to punish her for her own unhappiness.

I am speaking of the staging of the fake funeral, the astute response of "fantastic reason" to the violence tied to the passion of "stuff."

And so, in addition to the representation of

With *Kaos*, the Taviani brothers want to show the uncontainable strength of primary passions: ancestral terror, betrayer and betrayed maternity, erotic impulses.

I am speaking of forms of ritual spectacle: the dance where Sidora manifests the disruptive force of her unsated sensuality; the song of expectation of the full moon; the dance of the laborers around the jar; the evocation, almost in ballad form, of Garibaldi's passage into Sicily; the staging of the sorcery of miraculous glue.

I am speaking of iconography that conveys a

the natural need for and the violence of elementary passions, we have the staging of fantastic activity, through which the man dominates, representing both natural necessity and passions. And it is clearly no accident that the characters often make public the ritual spectacle they have produced through the establishment of the character as an "observer in the picture," or through the construction, through the movie camera, of a sort of "invisible spectator" who represents the echo or extension of the character/spectator.

In this way, the Sicilian landscape becomes not only the place and the iconographic equivalent of the realm of natural necessity and the passions, but also the scene that conveys symbolic forms and rituals, which lead man beyond the threshold of a brute natural state.

In the episode *Conversation with my Mother*, Pirandello, "the artist perplexed and withdrawn into himself like a fist", gets over the misfortunes of life thanks to the magic of memories. In this case the tendency of the authors to solve the situations with stylised and emblematic gestures grows stronger.

Similar to what happens in exemplary fashion in the prologue, where the crow evolves from being an object of bestial cruelty for the shepherds, to being a source of esthetic enchantment and conveyer of a superior point of view.

But *Kaos* also has an epilogue, the *Conversation with Mother*, which brings Pirandello himself directly into the scene, tired and forgetful—the image of the "perplexed artist" upon his return to Grigenti, his paternal home. I believe this is the finest moment of the film, and also one of the finest moments in recent Italian cinema. The mother, evoked by the suggestion of the place and the hour, exhorts her son, who is wounded by the "pain of existence," to know how to live like an open and outstretched hand and not always a clenched fist; to learn to "look at things, even with the eyes of one who no longer sees them." And the glance of the elderly writer truly succeeds in uniting with the enchanted glance of the mother as a child, in bringing to life, on the sea, the large red sail that had brought his glance—like that of Ulysses on his final voyage—to the discovery of the mysterious splendor of the white island and the happy intoxication of flight, depicted in those outstretched arms projected against the sky. Such gestures are constants in the Taviani's path toward iconographic stylization and "gestural theatricality," for instance, the gesture of hugging one's knees or crossing ones hands.

But beyond the great expressive power of this ending, what can be the meaning of this joining of the elegiac theme—the revival of the Stage of memory that becomes absolute lyrical image and inverted sign of the torment of the "perplexed artist"—to the representation of forms and rituals in which the conflicts and impulses of a primitive and archaic world are sublimated? I believe the meaning of this juxtaposition consists in the confirmation of the fact that the path towards the classicism of representation—theatricalized, ritualized, iconographically stylized—is not accomplished without a foundation of problematic self-reflectivity. It does not take place in the illusion that the problems and crisis of the "impassioned hero" has opened can be discharged in the search for the "Beautiful." If the "Viconian fantasy" represents the nascent state of art, culture, and human history, the glance of the "perplexed Artist"—in ironic or tormented fashion—

Good Morning Babylon: in the tragic and magic ending the cinema becomes a promise of immortality for the two dying brothers.

Facing page, from the top:

Bonanno, the heir of the builders of the cathedrals, in front of the Duomo of Pisa, considered as the "church of miracles".

Griffith, the builder of the "new cathedral", the cinema, on the set of *Intolerance*.

The magic of vision reveals itself also in these moments of figurative grace and choreographic lightness.

represents its flaw and decline. The power, profundity, and vitality of the Taviani brothers' research lies precisely here, in the way they hold the tension open to self-verification, which can be translated into formal splendor and yet can continue to act, like a woodworm that continues to nibble, and that thus prevents the Form from freezing into immobile, inert, academic beauty. And it is always the same tension that prevents the positive epilogue in this and other films, the very "spirit of the fable and of the enchanted glance" from being reduced to an edifying discourse. Clearly the Taviani brothers, and we,

are well aware that this danger is always imminent, and that there is always a risk that, in the search for Form, the spirit of Narcissus once again will insinuate itself.

With *Good Morning Babylon* (1987) the brothers push further along in the territory of self- reflection, which becomes explicit and almost autobiographical.

Again we have a fable—although the ending is apparently tragic, though made positive by the promise of immortality that Cinema ensures to the two brothers who are the tale's protagonists.

This may even be the representation of a dream, as one might deduce from the unreal scene at the end. It is a fable conducted with full narrative ease, a quilt of moments where the enchanted vision displays its ability to bring to the surface marvelous apparitions: the initial image of the Church of Miracles, the nocturnal view of New York, the great white elephant, rearing up in the middle of the woods.

And a tendency toward iconographic stylization also is confirmed. Representative gestures or postures: the palms of open hands, raised in a gesture of benediction, that the father turns toward his sons, and the same gesture they reciprocally make before their deaths; hands on head, as a sign of protection and comfort; fists that squeeze and support the chin, to hold in grief. There are openings onto and suspensions over the landscape. There are geometric plays of the movie camera, based on unexpected distancings—orthogonal angulations and variations that accomplish another variant of the framing effect and that often also govern the play of viewpoints, as in the wedding banquet sequence, where different perspectives follow one after another and are composed, as in a fresco in the grand Italian pictorial tradition.

These scenes confirm the increasing investigation of stylised figures, fixed in symbolic positions.

But, clearly, the most characteristic aspect of the film is the discourse on cinema and its nature as heir to the great Italian Medieval and Renaissance tradition in art, the "cathedral of our time," as Griffith is made to say in the film, but also the result of a "mode of production" that has to be that of the "artisan workshop," where "collective authorship" has not yet turned into alienating division of labor.

This revival of a theme that has been a constant in their work, since *Subversives*—a theme tied to considerations of the "craft of cinema," and its transformation into the "message" entrusted to the film—contains the greatest degree of meta-cinematographic reflection in the Taviani's work. But this is also the point they cannot move beyond without running the risk that their self-reflection will be overturned into a consolatory, edifying version that will re-emerge as petit-bourgeois ideology. Were this to happen, it would "reverse the wheel of history," with an apology for their "Tuscan-ness" proposed as a superior "mode of production," and no longer as a memory of a grand artistic tradition. The risk is that, in this no longer problematic combination of the "spirit of the Fable" and the self-reflective dimension, all polarities, all tensions, all productive lacerations disappear.

THE LANDSCAPE AS SOURCE OF BEAUTY AND MASK OF DEATH

For this discussion we need to travel along that earlier path, one that was barely followed with *The Meadow* and then abandoned. We need to go back to look within the passions that burn Prometheus; behind the figurative splendor of the landscape. It is a landscape that is increasingly modeled on the great Tuscan pictorial tradition, and we need to look beyond it, to the dark side of the moon, the image of Thanatos, which secretly always accompanies Orpheus on his journey, which is always hidden within the landscape of the fable.

This is the new stage of the Taviani's voyage and it includes three films from the Nineties: *Night Sun* (1990), *Fiorile* (1993), and *Elective Affinites* (1996). It is a stage that—despite the difficulty one sometimes senses in having the new discourse on the radicality of the passions coexist with a fully liberated figurative mastery, a difficulty in giving the discourse itself an energy equal to the splendor of the images— demonstrates the vitality and problematic nature of an artistic and intellectual experience, and the authors' capacity to put themselves back into play. Thus accusations of literary and figurative Mannerism seem ungenerous—indictments handed down by critics who are suspicious of literary (Tolstoy, Pirandello, Goethe) and figurative predilections, which are seen as external embellishments, as maskings of a discourse that seems to have become bloodless.

Night Sun, 1990, was freely inspired by Tolstoy's *Father Sergius*, one of the authors' great points of literary reference. It is the story of the Baron Sergio Giuramondo, a cadet and then envied attendant to King Charles III de Bourbon, who takes a liking to him and offers a fine match in marriage. But the King really deceives the young man, for the intended bride has been the King's lover. Deluded in love and humiliated, his ferocious pride brutally wounded, Sergio leaves Naples and the military life to become a monk. But he encounters yet another world of fiction, this time it is the Church. It deludes him, using him as a showy pretense to be placed on exhibition. Then he becomes a hermit on Mount Petra, where he cuts off his finger to resist the advances of Aurelia, who has climbed up to his refuge,

hoping to tempt him in order to win a bet. His fame grows, and following his odor of sanctity and miracle, the church once again tries to turn him into a hero to be on exhibition. Sergio now begins to yield to the enticements of fame and finally gives in to Matilda, a mentally unbalanced adolescent. Desperate, Sergio attempts suicide, by hurling himself into a lake, but he fails. Giving up the religious life, he returns to his childhood town, looking for an elderly couple who had asked him for the miracle of letting them die together. A peasant who doesn't recognize him but takes pity tells him that, in fact, the couple has died together. Sergio, finally liberated from the weight of his pride, wanders anonymously among these simple people, all traces of his past life having vanished.

This is a return to the "issue of competence," now configured in the form of a mythical tale, a folk tale. The end of Sergio's story is told to us in the voice of the peasant, projected in flashback onto the story. It is granted the warmth of collective memory, of the fable, just as the tree to which Sergio turns in three crucial moments of his life belongs to the universe. But what is important, for me, is the fact that the Taviani brothers have felt the need to give a

Night Sun. The harsh landscape of the central Appennino, the lawn with the blooming tree of happy childhood, the court of intrigue, betrayal and worldly vanity, the hermitage with the votive tree represent for father Sergio the places of his trials and setbacks.

new vitality to their discourse. They have staged a new variant of the figure of Prometheus who is no longer the builder of a new world, but the prideful seeker of Truth struggling against the Deceiver. And the Deceiver is now worldly, political, or religious power, the realm of appearance and fiction, and Prometheus is trying to turn himself, his very existence, into the embodied negation of that world. Father Sergio's quest develops along a path that, as in folk tales or myths, traverses various spaces, true "spaces of Trial": the worldly spaces of the Bourbon Court and the official Church, the space of the Hermitage; the space of authenticity and moral rigor against the harsh Apennine landscape. And, as in the simpler model of the folk tale, the image of the Antagonist, the force that opposes the Hero's project has a body, here, literally, the body of the woman, of femininity, the image and source of Deception and Temptation. Nonetheless the Woman is only the apparent image of the Deceiver. When the final recognition has taken place, the Subject returns to discover in himself, in his own pride, in his "passion for self," the enemy that kept him from the Truth. It is an enemy that one can vanquish only by losing one's own identity in anonymity,

in a negation of self. This is the definitive reckoning with the figure of Prometheus/Narcissus. It is not a Manneristic return, but rather a sign that the authors' quest is no longer satisfied by the discovery of the spirit of the Fable. They are no longer satisfied by the enchanted Vision, or the virtue of Art, and its capacity to redeem the sorrow that is present in existence and in the history.

Fiorile was made in 1993. A French car emerges from a tunnel into the light of the Tuscan countryside ("What is that light down there?" asks a child's voice. "It is Tuscany," responds a man). A family with the Italian name Benedetti is traveling in the car and, at their first stop, the two children learn that their name bears and ancient curse, tied to a story of love, money, and death. The tale begins two centuries earlier, at the time of the Napoleonic campaigns. The father begins to tell them the love story of Jean and Elisabetta—who will be Fiorile to him, the name of the beauty of his ideals and his love. Distracted by his love for her, Jean loses track of his regiment's gold, that he was entrusted to guard, and the treasure is stolen by Elisabetta's brother, Corrado. As a result, Jean is condemned to death. One

Defeated temptation: Sergio (Julian Sands) rejects Aurelia.

Victorious temptation: Sergio yelds to the girl (Charlotte Gainsborough). The true reason of Sergio's defeat lies in the pride that still burns him, in the Promethean will to become a saint.

hundred years later the curse tied to that gold returns to strike Elisa, the descendent of Fiorile, who, because of her brother's ambition, is condemned to despair over a lost love, a young peasant who is forced to emigrate to Argentina. When the new Fiorile learns of this, she takes tremendous revenge and poisons the brothers who have betrayed and deceived her. She does this during a voyage to Volterra, undertaken to rid herself of the child she is carrying which, instead, is born. One generation later, a third Benedetti is struck by the curse of the gold. Massimo, a law student, follows his girlfriend into the partisan struggle. He is arrested in their first action and is the only one whose life is spared, only because of the name he bears, which makes him cursed by the people of his region. His lover, who is expecting a child, is arrested by the Fascists and dies in prison, after giving birth. Massimo goes on to live alone, considered crazy by everyone, and sends his son to live in France, far from the homeland of the curse. The man driving the car is that son, Luigi, who is returning to find his father. Incredulous of the legend of the "Benedetti, Maledetti" [12], he is taking his two children, descendants of Corrado and Fiorile, to meet

their grandfather and to confront their roots. However, the tragic shadow of the ancient legend extends to distant places, and Luigi tells his wife he no longer wants to return there. But the curse already has already left its mark. The hand of the daughter writes the name of Fiorile on the misted over window of the car, while the son grips a golden coin tightly in his fist.

Thus *Fiorile* is also a return, but not only a thematic one. It is a return to the Tuscan landscape, the landscape of Pontassieve, in the province of Florence, with its meadows bursting with the colors if juniper and lavender, with the rows of cypress trees along the distant outlines of the hills. And then there is the landscape constructed by man, the Medici villas (here it is the Villa La Pietraia), the Piazza della Santissima Annunziata, as well as the farmhouses and barns. Finally, there is the "human landscape," made up of figures, faces, and ancient gestures. It is a return to the tale filtered through the memory and legends created and passed down over the centuries by folk tradition.

Thus it would seem to be a return to the spirit of the Fable and the Enchanted Vision. It is not only the narrating voice of the father that evokes the three episodes of the past, it is also

[12] Benedetti is the surname of the protagonist, but in Italian also means "blessed" and is used in contrapposition with "maledetti", which means "cursed".

Fiorile. The lawns, the Ville Medicee, the celebrated squares: in those places the tragic events caused by the passions oppose and live together with the beauty of the landscape and the tradition of the Tuscan culture.

the enchanted glance of the children, which almost seems to allow them to be reborn from the space they are traversing. It is an enchanted glance that continues into a suspended and almost magical glance that governs the movements of the movie camera at every start.

It would seem to be a return to a happy, solar vision of the landscape and of the values it conveys. One would think this, observing the way the camera lingers on the smiling faces of the women in love, on the graceful gestures (the mutual kissing of hands of Jean and Fiorile

when they meet), the long fields that overtake and disperse the figures and the action, and in the contemplation of this landscape of Leonardo da Vinci.

Clearly the landscape is the place of Beauty, of Art that mimics, captures in images, and transfigures nature. But Beauty, which exists and which the glance knows how to capture, is no longer capable of transfiguring events, even dramatic ones, and inverting their meaning, as it did in *The Night of the Shooting Stars.* This is a negative fable, where malicious passions (for gold, for power) inescapably oppose the

These two pages:
Fiorile. Gestures
and attitudes full
of grace....

passions of love, converting them into hatred and destructive vendetta. They obsessively negate pietas, extending their shadow from the past to the present. And, in *Fiorile*, as in The *Meadow*, death hides behind beauty, and the space of the landscape is experienced as the container and source of the sense of destruction and ambiguity of the passions. These are the passions of love and money, the passion of the cruelty of family affections and the capacity to betray that hides, even in blood ties.

Tragic meaning generated by contemplation of the passions is conjoined with a reflection on the landscape and its role in the destiny of the characters and of man. This is manifested even more explicitly in the final film in this cycle, *Elective Affinities* (1996), a confrontation with Goethe's great novel, something the brothers had always thought about. Once again, as always in the Taviani's confrontation with literary points of reference, this is not an adaptation but a work freely inspired by a novel. They take poetic and conceptual suggestions from Goethe, but only to orient and lead them around their discourse. It is a work of

appropriation that, in this case, becomes evident in the Italian setting, in Tuscany above all and then in Venice, and in Rome. But it is also evident in the elimination of the "social" portion of the novel and in the reduction and transformation of the portion related to the

...and images and gestures of the evil passions, of hate, eagerness, deception.

***Elective Affinitives.
The new temptation
of Utopia: to rule
nature…***

"construction of the landscape," where Carlotta is the main protagonist in Goethe's novel. Thus it would be of little use to pursue a debate that stems from comparisons with the literary reference. What is interesting, however, is to see the way in which—in the story of Carlotta and Ottilia, Edoardo and Ottone; in the tragic failure of their attempt to program their passions—this film continues the discourse on the landscape as

both a source of Beauty and a container of deadly passions.

It seems that the landscape is no longer only a place of Beauty and mask of Death, as in *Fiorile,* but the direct Antagonist of the characters. It is the manifestation of a Nature that doesn't yield to Man's plans for his Passions and that exacts revenge, injuring to the death those who would challenge it. This new role can

...to rule passions.

Once again the splendor of the Tuscan architectural culture: the villa of Poggio a Caiano.

be seen in the image of the hostile fixity of the pool that the four protagonists contemplate at the beginning of their plan. It will be the origin of the first of the tragic events in which their existence will be swept along. In this new role, the landscape has an obsessive presence, also manifested through its ability to penetrate the interiors, affecting their light and color.

At the same time there is a continued and reinforced exaltation of Beauty, that of the churches, cities, and villas of Tuscany. There is continued and greater stylization, in the geometrical, compositional, and figural organization that is created through a series of "symbolic spatial arrangements" and iterated positions (women kneeling and embracing the bellies of other women, crossed hands, etc.). This is also achieved through an accentuation of the symbolic value of color, which charges places and bodies with meaning. It is as if the more one has a sense of the deadly role played by Nature and the Passions, the more one feels the need to compose the noble representations of men in stylized and symbolic images.

In this sense, *Elective Affinities* is truly a key work. It picks up the threads of the discourse and seeks to compose a new equilibrium for the polarities that have now come completely to

This page and the next two: In *Elective Affinities* the search for symbolic spatial arrangements, for repeated stylised positions reaches its climax: a woman kneeling and embracing the belly of another woman, crossing and shaking hands, symbolic gestures of affection and love, joined hands expressing grief.

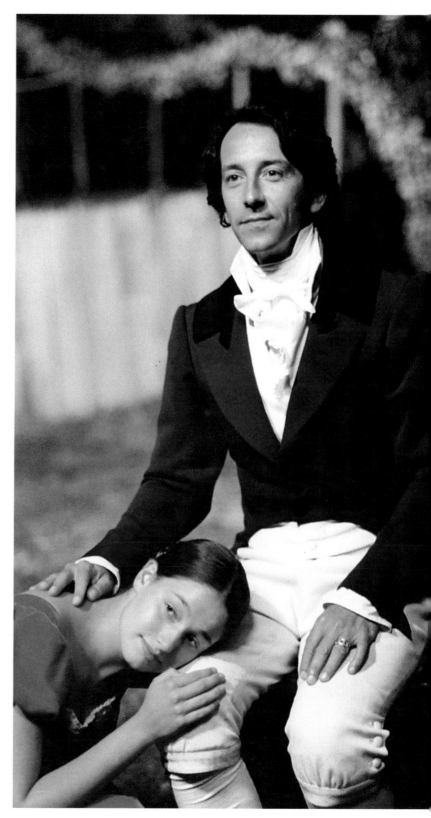

light. This is a polarity between an increasingly revealed formal knowledge of representation and an awareness of the radicality of the evil of existence. This is expressed at the end of the film, in the animal cry of the servant girl who is lost in the impenetrable indifference of the figurative splendor of the Tuscan landscape.

TU RIDI: THE VIOLENT VULGARITY OF TODAY'S HISTORY AND THE CONSOLATION OF ART, BUT ONLY AFTER LIFE

With *Tu ridi* (1998), the Tavianis return to "their" Pirandello and also to Rome, Sicily, and contemporary life.

In its current version, the film consists of two parts. The first, Felice, represents the original synthesis of three Pirandello short stories. *Tu ridi* (1912) is inspired by the story of a gray little man. He is frustrated at having had to interrupt a brilliant career as an opera singer, he is unresigned to his day job as a book-keeper, and wrenched awake at night by a jealous wife who misinterprets his nocturnal laughing. Felice himself discovers that his strange laughing is tied to a dream of an atrocious hoax at the expense of his friend, Tobia. *The Imbecile* (1912) is the

inspiration for the portion of the story where Felice avenges his friend's suicide. *Sun and Shade* (1896) loosely inspires the final part of the episode, with the trip to the sea, the encounter with Nora, the final triumphant opera performance, and the suicide in the sea. The second part of the film, entitled *Two Kidnappings*, is inspired by *The Capture* (1918), which sets the story of the long ago kidnapping of the elderly doctor Ballarò within a Mafia abduction. The latter crime, inspired by current events, concludes ferociously with the killing of a child whose body is then dumped into acid.

Originally the film was to have had a first section, The *Daughter*, in which the Taviani brothers reconstructed two episodes from the life of Pirandello. One was the triumphant evening when he received the Nobel prize, and the other, many years earlier, was the fiasco and harsh critical reception of Six Characters in Search of an Author, a rejection that wounded both the writer and his daughter Lietta. As the Taviani brothers imagine it, it was on that very night, as a sign of revolt and compensation, that Pirandello set down to write Felice. Indeed the episode is introduced by a voiceover by the writer. The function of this first episode was, I

Tu ridi. Felice triumphing just before his death: comfort and salvation thanks to music and art.

The old Ballarò, thanks to the superiority of his "knowledge", can discover—just before his death—the happiness of a smiling young woman, of a caress to her face.

Facing page: Art (the fresco by Giotto re-created by computer, the dance) moves also into the cruel story of the child and his murderer.

think, to clarify the fact that one of the themes of the film is a reflection on the role of the Author, on the relationship between life and art, and on the nature of humor[13] and comedy.

Stefano Socci has dwelt at length on the particular nature of the relationship between this film and Pirandello. For my part, however, I would like to try to see how *Tu ridi* fits into the line of discourse that I have developed in the preceding pages. I would like to examine it especially in terms of the relationship between Art, Nature, and History and the irreconcilable duality between the recognition of Beauty and

the inescapable tragic sense of existence that lurks in the harsh Nature that lies within and outside us.

Here the presence of art and its role are explicitly made into a theme. This occurs in the initial motivation of the Felice episode, an echo or trace of which remains in the activity of the narrator's voice. It also happens in the passages of the triumphant past that Felice futilely tries to hold onto. And it occurs in the final triumph, where the character's passion for song overcomes his fear of illness and death and, above all, restores order to his world and returns

[13] In addition to Socci's essay in this volume, see Alberto Cattini's introduction to the screenplay for *Tu ridi*, Mantua, 1999.

him to a reconciled vision of life and affections. In this vision, his friend Tobia is alive and witnesses his victory, as does his wife Erika, with her new husband. The arrogant impresario is gone, humiliated, mocked even by his hangers-on. In the episode of Ballarò, art is the colored glass that lets one look at things and the miserable life they represent in a new way. This is the superiority of "knowing," which converts the drama into smiles and games. In the Mafia episode, art takes the form of the painting of Giotto, which Vincenzo recreates with his computer, but it is also the archaic dance of his assassin.

The human value of art is one of the grand themes that traverses this film and is one of its unifying elements. If there is something new, a departure for the two authors, it is their focus on contemporary life, on the world of today; on the violence that is intrinsic to that life, and on its vulgarity. Contemporary life is not only that of the barbaric Mafioso crime. It is also the world where Felice and Tobia live and are humiliated by an arrogant and violent vulgarity, which the Taviani see as predominant in today's Italy. The similarities emerge, between what already is, what will be, and what was long ago.

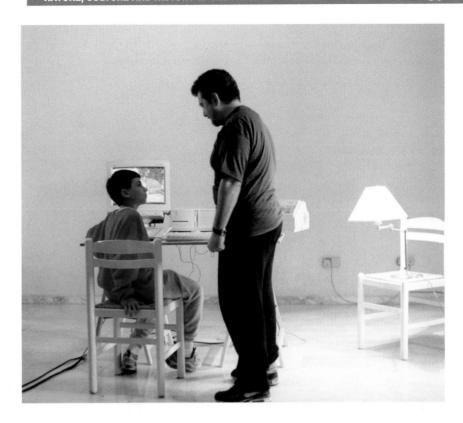

What is important is that the authors have ceased contemplating an atemporal reality where the recognition and construction of Beauty is opposed to the evil and deadly character of Nature and the Passions. They have gone back to History—to measure the efficacy of Art in history, in the concrete and everyday life of men today, with the possibility of transforming and redeeming it.

Nonetheless, Art can no longer prefigure Utopia, nor can it undo the tragedies of history through happy stories.

After the illusion of art, the consciousness of the end "in the bottom of the sea".

In *Tu ridi*, in the world of Felice and the unfortunate Vincenzo, which is no longer the world of Ballarò, Art can console the unhappiness of life only if it is coupled with an awareness of the need for death. It is only in his acceptance of death, of his voyage "into the depths of the sea" that Felice can forever realize his triumph. And Vincenzo entrusts to Giotto's Art, to his sorrowful Angel, not his salvation, which he knows is impossible, but his memory.

In the Taviani's work, *Tu ridi* seems to represent a moment of definitive predominance by the dark side of their view of the world, a surrender to Sorrow.

And yet, in their glance that returns to face today's world, one senses a shudder of rebellion. And their discourse continues, as does their desire to speak to the public with their stories and with their images, not to be content with a quest for an immobile and inert Beauty, but to find motivations and forms to still communicate.

WAITING FOR *RESURRECTION*

This is perhaps where the new discourse on *Resurrection* begins.

It is difficult and perhaps also unjust to speak

about a film before seeing it, before it has even been completed, on the basis of some statements gleaned here and there, from an interview, albeit certainly long and significant,[14] and, finally, on the basis of one version of the

After the game, the atrocious crime.

---

[14] *Taviani. Dalla Russia con amore*, interview with Lietta Tornabuoni in "La Stampa".

screenplay. There is a risk of forcing an analysis that doesn't take into consideration the concreteness of the text or the shots that photographs on the set can only partially intuit. It leaves out the film's rhythm and music, so important, as always, in the brothers' work.[15] Yet we have an awareness that comes from the path we have followed, along with the two authors, film after film, choice after choice, which compels us to form certain opinions.

Resurrection is a return to Tolstoy, the late Tolstoy. The novel was written, with great effort, between 1889 and 1899. (The two Tolstoy stories

Divine and Human and *Father Sergius*, which inspired St. Michael had a Rooster and Night Sun also are from Tolstoy's late period.) During these ten tormented years, the great Russian writer decided to develop a true story that his friend Koni had told him and that reminded him of an event from his youth (the seduction of Gaša, a young maid). He undertook this project in order to finance the duchobory sect, which the writer had taken to heart during that period. These are years of profound crisis and change, in terms of political and religious convictions, and in terms of his ideas about the role of art. Indeed *What is*

Resurrection.
Katiuscia is taken
to the trial.

[15] For the role of music in the Taviani's films, see R. La Rochelle, *Il regista e la musica da film: una testimonianza dei fratelli Taviani.* In *Enciclopedia della musica. Il Novecento,* Einaudi, Turin, 2001, pp.649-663.

Dimitri with the Neva in the background.

The Court of Appeal, scene of the last, futile attempt to save Katiuscia from being deported to Siberia.

Art? is dated 1897, and in it Tolstoy affirms that art must be "a tool for transferring the Christian religious conscience from the field of reason and intellect to the domain of feelings. Thus it must bring men near to that ideal of life, to that perfection and unity that are indicated to him by his religious conscience."[16] Strangely, at least at first glance, it is not Tolstoy the utopian and messianic prophet in *Resurrection*, especially in its ending, that interests the Taviani brothers. Instead it is the "extremely grand Tolstoyan sense of spectacle in the use of the "love story" genre (in the manner of *Doctor Zhivago*, or even *Chains* or *Torment*)."[17] In other words, their attention is turned not to the social novel, but "instead to the passionate love story, to the great sentiments, strong intensity; the pleasure of describing grand spaces, and man in nature and

[16] L. Tolstoy, *Che cosa è l'arte (What is art?)*, Italian translation, Feltinelli, Milan, 1978, p. 191.

[17] Interview with Lietta Tornabuoni, op. cit.

Dimitri sees the sufferings of the convicts.

in History, and to the desire to reach a vast public." For this reason, in the film the "social" part is reduced to the encounter where Prince Dimitri cedes his lands to the peasants after

The memory of Katiuscia's seduction and of her despair.

Top: Dimitri confesses to his wet-nurse that he wants to marry Katiuscia in expiation of his guilt, even if he does not really love her. Above and next page: Dimitri gives his land to the peasants.

having conquered their suspicions. and great space is given to the story of Dimitri and Katiuscia. The plot is well known, even if, according to critics and this author, it is not completely justified and resolved. It is a story about the anxiety of redemption and expiation that strikes Dimitri Nechliudov—a spoiled and insensitive nobleman, who has abandoned the ideals of his youth—when, as a judge of the people, a prostitute, accused of complicity in a murder, is brought before him. He recognizes her as a girl he was in love with many years before and who, pushed by his "animal spirit," he had seduced and paid off with one hundred rubles. He tries to have her acquitted and, failing in this, he follows her to Siberia and asks her to marry him, although he doesn't love her. She, however, turns him down, precisely because she has come to love him again.

I said earlier that the distancing from the "political" Tolstoy is seen above all in the ending. In the novel, after Dimitri bids farewell to Katiuscia, who "no longer had need of him," he is tormented by visions of the terrible evil he has seen in prison and looks for an answer in passages of the Gospel of Matthew. In the beginning, he finds the answers based on piety,

forgiveness, the refusal to condemn the guilty, and, to be simplistic, turning the other cheek ("But is it possible that this is all there is?"). He understands that it is precisely this way. "It happened that an idea, which appeared strange to him earlier, like a paradox, even like a joke, increasingly found confirmation in life, and suddenly he felt that he was faced with an extremely simple, unquestionable truth. And so

the idea was now clear to him, that the only and indubitable means of salvation from the terrifying evil from which men suffered consisted solely in this, that men had to always recognize themselves as guilty before God and therefore incapable of punishing or correcting other men, Look for the kingdom of God and his justice, and all the rest will come to you and more. We, instead, go looking for the rest, and it

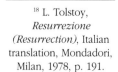
Mariette: Dimitri must renounce this new love.

is obvious that we are not finding it. 'Here then, is my new life task. One has just ended, and another is beginning.'"[18]

The film completely renounces the discovery of the Gospel at the end, although it does not renounce the prospect of renewal for the main character. Dimitri allows the train, which should have taken him back to Moscow and to his previous life, to depart. He then is drawn into an izba (a traditional log house in rural Russia), illuminated and decorated for a party by a group of young people who are celebrating the arrival of the new century. He becomes involved and moved by their expectation, full of hope, and by the love that seems to fill their lives, to the point where he says that his hope is to "love as you

[18] L. Tolstoy, *Resurrezione (Resurrection)*, Italian translation, Mondadori, Milan, 1978, p. 191.

love each other." From this perspective, with this hope, he prepares to live in the century that is arriving, the TWENTIETH CENTURY, as it appears in large writing, in the Futurist characters of the Russian avant-garde, which concludes the film.

And so there are two completely different endings, the importance of which cannot be overstated. If it is true that the two brothers cannot share the precise content of Tolstoy's utopia, Tolstoy still remains for them "the father, the older brother, the son," the point of reference in their representation of "life in its essence," and in their search for and "reaffirmation of lost values."[19] He is there in their capacity for renewal, their ability to begin again from the beginning, with a passion that restores and opens up to the future and to men. This seems to be the deepest, most vital, and most universal core of Tolstoy's utopia.

It is within this context, I believe, that their return to the "spirit of the tale" should be understood. This should be the basis for interpreting their desire to follow the great Russian writer in their use of the "love story genre," in their choice to entrust the discourse's ability to communicate to the representation of

grand emotions, grand passions, and grand settings. And this should be the basis for understanding their decision to turn to a medium, television, which can reach millions of people.

This development in their work, in other

Talking in confidence.

[19] Interview with Lietta Tornabuoni, op. cit.

Dimitri has decided: "Farewell to old life...". The trip towards Siberia: once again, violence for Katiuscia, and now also for Dimitri.

words, seems to intuit that the representation of beauty—previously visible in their images of landscapes, faces, gestures, attitudes and positions figuratively frozen by the esthetic act that contemplates and cleanses—will return to encounter an open attitude to the life force and to man's story, to a new century that is about to arrive. Doubts can become insinuated and can

ironically overturn the discourse. The century awaited is the one we have already lived through. It was the "brief century," the century "of wars and revolutions," the century that brought both great hope and an assault on the sky that, when it failed and had to look back to a time, we still don't know how far back, was overturned and transformed into a tragic lie.

The party in the isba to celebrate the arrival of the new century.

Paolo and Vittorio
Taviani on the set
of *Good Morning
Babylon*.

SANDRO BERNARDI

TUSCAN LANDSCAPES

Tuscany dwells within us in the films of Paolo and Vittoria Taviani. One could, or one ought to say that it is almost the protagonist of the micro-text that their films constitute as a whole. Sometimes it is present directly, at other times indirectly, and sometimes it is absent only because it is best to merely sense its air, its power. As early as 1967, at the time of *Subversives*, Grazzini observed that there was a profound tie between the two directors and their land, the relationship between their sanguine, strong, hard nature, and Tuscany. "They have in their blood, and their land does not lie, a harshness of impression, a disdainful edge, an ear to the ground, that gives their work a pungent taste, something off-putting: the coldness of truth, the rejection of manners. There are few directors in Italy who, like the Taviani, focus on the truth,

without concessions to spectacular frills."[1]

Moreover, their love for Tuscany is tied to a revival of tradition. One could say, paraphrasing a poem by Pasolini, that the Taviani are subversives because they are conservatives, because their love lies only in tradition. As Riccardi Ferrucci has observed: "the mechanism of the Taviani's cinema proceeds precisely from their recovery of the past, from stories heard by the hearth, from rural legends, old proverbs."[2] The occasional extras, such as the one in *Padre Padrone* (1977), or in *Subversives*, if only for the presence of Leonardo Da Vinci, are confirmations of the need to return as soon as possible to their homeland, if only in thought. But the landscape's absence is also significant, and journeys far away from Tuscany always lead to strong, and hard lands, equally harsh if not more so: the Sardinia

[1] G. Grazzini, in *Corriere della Sera*, September 8, 1967.
[2] See R. Ferrucci, P. Turini, *Poetry of Italian Landscape*, p. 13.

of *Padre Padrone*, the Sicily of *A Man for Burning* or *Kaos*, the South of *Allonsanfan* or *Night Sun*, the bitter America of *Good Morning Babylon*. Tuscany is the backdrop for one episode from the film *Marriage Outlaws*, which shows the enigmatic sets for the large piazza and cathedral of Massa Marittima. The metaphorical, enigmatic film *Under the Sign of the Scorpion* was shot in Tuscany, set in a mysterious prehistoric time, and filmed in the park of the Uccellina. The buildings of Pisorno, in Tuscany, are the starting point for the story of *Good Morning Babylon*.

But, to avoid a banal inventory, I would like to dwell only on some of their films, those that are set completely in Tuscany: *Night of the Shooting Stars*, *The Meadow*, *Fiorile*, and *Elective Affinities*. These four films, while telling profoundly different stories and set in very different times, share the mysterious cruelty of the Tuscan earth.

TUSCANY AS A LAND BOTH YOUNG AND ANCIENT

Let us turn to one of the strangest and most enigmatic of the Taviani films, one for which they also produced the treatment and screenplay that, therefore, allows us to better understand the profound relationship between these two Tuscan

masters of cinema and their native land. Here, Tuscany plays a truly mysterious role: a solar land, open and generous on the one hand; dark and disturbing on the other. San Gimignano and its mythical towers have been utilized numerous times in European and American cinema as a stereotype for the medieval setting. Here, however, it loses its entire traditional, folkloristic character, and becomes a town suspended between past and present, between reality and fable, adapted for dreaming and staging the terrible tale of the Pied Piper of Hamelin. *The Meadow* is a complete interweaving of history and sites, so that telling the story without describing the sites would make no sense. Nor would it be meaningful to show the sites without the story, because the former seem to acquire their profound ambiguity from the story, and vice versa, the story seems to emerge, with its disturbing quality, from the strange beauty of the sites. Thus we should proceed in parallel fashion, moving from descriptions to narration and back again.

A young, solitary, and melancholy student, Giovanni, goes to spend a few days at his parents' country house in San Gimignano. The town is presented through three wonderful shots:

from the summit of the hill, back-lit, and with a slow forward tracking shot taken from behind Giovanni, who is seated on the low wall of the ruined villa. This reveals the classical Tuscan landscape, with the street that runs directly off in space, to the horizon, as in a Quattrocento painting, winding and unwinding, up and down hills, amid cypress trees. They are images that not only serve to identify the town and the place, but also, from the very beginning, add something different to these famous and, by now, postcard-familiar places that cinema has always presented to us. They offer a dark aspect, like an impenetrable painting, radiant but also cruel. In fact, in the meadow that spreads out, sloping beneath the young man's feet, an animal moves about amid the grass and immediately disappears, just long enough to leave one wondering: was it a fox, or simply a rabbit? The animal runs away into the grass, but not without having made a strong impression on the young man, who is suffering from a sort of exhaustion brought about by the life he has led thus far in the city that he can no longer tolerate.

A voiceover recounts that the foxes of the area are ill with one of the most dangerous and frightening diseases, rabies. A shooting party is organized during which Giovanni manages to kill one of these mysterious, fascinating animals. That morning, at dawn, the hunters assemble right along the road that runs by Giovanni's house. At this spot, the Tuscan countryside seems simultaneously extremely vast and small, clustered around the young man's house, both distant and far, familiar and alien, disturbing. It is the true *unheimlich* space, as Freud would say. The hunters spread out in the meadow that seems immense, in an extremely long shot of the morning light. Day breaks. A panning shot of the meadow in close-up shows us the green and yellowish grass beneath the sun and, further away, the scattered men whose voices we can hear off screen. Giovanni stands in place at the edge of the woods, looking around passionately, moved by this adventure that is bringing him back to one of life's most archaic moments, man the hunter. The fox appears far off, at the end of a large meadow, stops for a moment at the edge of the woods, as if to observe him, or to look down at the ground. Giovanni, who has thought to himself: "I'll give a year of my life because a fox appears and I am the one who kills it," succeeds in hitting it. His secret promise proves immediately to be an authentic prophecy, as in

The Meadow. The first appearance of Eugenia (Isabella Rossellini) between the towers of San Gimignano.

fables of old. Giovanni shoots and the animal falls to the ground. The others converge from afar, among the trees. The adventure of the hunt—the evening party with the sounds of knives that compose a sort of archaic music to the ears of Giovanni, who is tired and half-asleep—leads us into the sort of trance within which the entire film will unfold. "All this," thinks Giovanni, looking back some days later, writing to his friend Leonardo, "all this was only a preparation for my encounter with Eugenia." She is a splendid girl, extremely sweet and melancholy, who appears the following day in the town piazza, seen from below, while walking on stilts. She is as tall as a bewitched character in a fairy tale, large but also delicate and fragile, struggling to balance her small body on the length of the stilts, which are hidden by a very long shirt. With a degree in anthropology and employed by the tax office in Florence, Eugenia lives only for the time she manages to devote to children, on Sundays, when she organizes lively public performances in the piazzas of the town. When Giovanni sees her, she is acting out the fable of the magical piper. So tall, amid the medieval buildings of the town, she truly has the air of a fairy tale character. During the enactment of the story of the Pied Piper, a storm suddenly erupts and as children and actors seek refuge in a school-studio, a bolt of lightning strikes a large oak tree that falls in front of the door. With Eugenia's help, the children act out a primordial representation of fear and, externalizing that emotion's most atavistic forms, they regress, freeing themselves in the most disturbing expressions until they achieve a collective liberation. It is a sort of Sabbath, a pandemonium of some monstrous archaic rite. When the rain passes, all the children, now cheerful, return home. The enchantment seems over, but Giovanni remains bewitched by the scene he has witnessed and by Eugenia's disquieting beauty.

Giovanni confesses to Eugenia that he is in love with her and talks about a film by Rossellini, *Germania anno zero.* He describes the film audience's dismay and tells her how, at the exit, he was greeted by someone he didn't know who, needed to speak to someone after the film's vision. The next day Eugenia will see the film and make love with Giovanni, but Eugenia also has another man. Enzo is a young dreamer who respects Eugenia's desires and accepts sharing her with another, even though it causes him great suffering. He also has a political project: he hopes to establish an agricultural commune on what are,

for the most part, uncultivated lands. Although in love with both men, and loved by both, Eugenia, begins to suffer. She cannot live with one or the other and the three young people feel as if their legs are broken, like wounded foxes. Their dreams of love and freedom, of a utopia (which is always present and alive in the Taviani's cinema) to be established through a new, free community, have now been shattered.

Toward the end, after having tried in vain to pursue the career of magistrate, which he had begun brilliantly, Giovanni returns to San Gimignano to greet Eugenia who is leaving for Algeria. He writes, once again, to his friend and describes the surrounding countryside, in a manner quite different from the enchantment, and the magic, with which he had seen it at the beginning of the film. Now it seems like a place of great suffering. While his voice reads the letter off screen, the camera lingers in a long, fixed shot on the meadow.

How could I write you, Leonardo, that this big valley appeared to me like a sign of happiness? How was I able to say that this meadow was beautiful? (foreground shot of the meadow). *The most sensitive parts of that flower are sucked out*

Giovanni, Eugenia and Enzo. Beyond the window, the square of San Gimignano.

The three characters on the lawn of their unsuccessful project.

One passionate moment of the relationship between Eugenia and Giovanni.

by the bees. The sun that had caused the daisies to bloom now spoils them. That tree is infested by a swarm of ants. This one by snails. That plant is in too much heat. This one in too much cold. Too dry, too damp, too much light, too much shade. Every meadow is a hospital and a hospital causes more suffering than a cemetery (now a slow panning shot reveals Giovanni from the back, looking out over the meadow. Eugenia approaches him from behind and embraces him.)

This discourse is a quotation of a wonderful passage by Giacomo Leopardi who, in *Zibaldone*, comments with these same words on nature's deceptive appearance, even in its moments of greatest luxuriance.

Enter a garden of plants, grasses, flowers. No matter how much you want to laugh. Even in the mildest season of the year. You can't turn your glance anywhere without finding privation (...) the sweet honey is not made by the industrious, patient, good, virtuous bees without unspeakable torments to those most delicate fibers, without pitiless massacres of flowerets. That tree is infested with a swarm of ants, that other one with caterpillars, flies, snails, mosquitoes (...). That

[3] Leopardi, *Zibaldone di pensieri*, pp. 4176-4177.

plant is too hot, this one too cold; too much light, too much shade, too humid, too dry (...) every garden is almost like a vast hospital (a place much more deplorable than a cemetery).[3]

Now we have come to the end. Bitten by a rabid dog, Giovanni dies in the helicopter that is taking him from San Gimignano to Bologna. The metaphor of the hospital shows how, even youth, beneath its veil of apparent perfection, hides profound suffering. If the nature around San Gimignano shows two faces, one happy and one sorrowful, like two aspects of the same meadow, the city seems no less ambiguous. Fully protected within its medieval towers, in its narrow and deserted streets, with people all closed off behind the shutters of medieval houses like many centuries ago, or with its small piazzas closed off between the fortified medieval buildings, its narrow windows and thick stone walls—San Gimignano is a symbol of the world where the ancient mixes with the modern, freedom with imprisonment, the picturesque with the gloomy, and where radiant aspects intersect with the sublime, forming dangerous perspectives. With its invisible inhabitants; its innumerable children that, drawn by the fable, follow the sweet

Eugenia; San Gimignano is also the mysterious city of the piper who, as Eugenia would like to do, draws away the children from the real world, to lead them toward the woods where they go, not to die, but to live, in a twist on the fairy tale's ending: "Later it became known that in the woods the children had become adults and were living in a just and happy community."

But this community, the utopian community that the three young people dream of building in the real world, is not possible, not only because of the injustice of others, but also the fault of the desires that divide us from each other. Youth, which is the age of utopia, is also the age of the greatest suffering, like the meadow during the summer, where everything seems joyously at peace and everything is in ferment and disturbed agitation. It is a film about the unhappiness of a generation that was deprived of its dreams, the generation of '68. *The Meadow* is also a film about the fractured dreams of all generations, a film about the mystery of nature and the sorrow that always and inexorably follows every search for happiness.

THE TUSCANY OF MYTH AND HISTORY

Another film, *Night of the Shooting Stars*, is equally mysterious, but in a different way.

History and Myth interweave to form a single narrative in the story of a terrible massacre that actually took place in San Miniato, the Taviani's birthplace. The events are seen through a child's eyes, like a fairy tale of old. It is a calm, star-filled night, August 10, the feast day of San Lorenzo. The duomo of Florence can be glimpsed through a bedroom window and a young mother tells her daughter the story of another Night of San Lorenzo, when she herself was a young child, in 1944. With her, we sink back into the past. A sudden cut takes us to a field, where an isolated tree trembles and shakes all its greenery at the rumble of distant bombs. A pear rolls to the ground amid the grass. According to archaic tradition the mythical tree in the middle of a clearing indicates a sacred place, now disturbed by the disruptions of History. The paradisiacal aspect of this sacred place—unexpectedly thrown into disarray by man, will never go back to what it was. In the distance we see the blue Tuscan hills, also apparently serene, a sweetness that will soon be bathed in the blood of a fratricidal war. From below, a pile of hay apparently hides a refugee; the man comes forth, emerging from the very womb of mother earth as if in a second birth.

The entire film is dense with landscape images that take on an intimate, profound, and archaic religious and mythical sense. Indeed, as in a second birth, the man undresses as two women arrive bearing new party clothes. It seems like a ritual, but instead it is a very simple story. Corrado, the protagonist, comes out of hiding to marry Bellindia, the pregnant girl who awaits him a short distance away, in a group. Wearing their Sunday best, the small wedding procession walks along a country path toward a solitary little church. This too is a painting: the small solitary church in the Tuscan hills, symbol of peace and silence. But inside, life is by no means tranquil. The priest celebrating the marriage is breathless, dirty, and hurried, he seems to be foreseeing the end of the world and speaks of the Wrathful God of the Apocalypse that is about to arrive. In church, the small group of people witnessing the wedding includes a young girl, the little Cecilia who, drawn by the words of the priest, absent-mindedly turns to a painting on the church wall, observing the devils, the flames, and the serpents, in a popular inferno that is both grotesque and childlike. Outside, a little while later, in the churchyard of the poor country church, the small group of peasants stops to offer a simple

Solidarity during the work in the country, before the battle. An excellent depiction of the Tuscan landscape.

Facing page: The episode of the country wedding in *The Night of the Shooting Stars*. In the background, a view of San Miniato.

celebration to the newlyweds, with a bit of bread and glasses of wine. A balladeer intones a few verses from the *Iliad* that will prove to be prophetic: "Smile Hector…" It is the scene from the Trojan War where Hector, before going off to battle to die at the hand of Achilles, lifts up his little son Astyanax and calls upon the gods to protect him. Meanwhile, we are given another sign of fear and disorder: a young unknown man runs through the fields in the hills, hunted by enemies; he races toward San Miniato, which is seen in the distance with its red tower of Frederick II of Swebia. Who might this be? We

don't know, and the scene stops here, like a painting that poses a mystery, an open question; a landscape where men are hunted down.

Now we are in San Miniato (which in the film is called San Martino). We see the deserted streets, the desolate town piazza, a group of frightened people who seek refuge in an entranceway. The town is terrorized, it is occupied by the Germans and the Americans are supposed to be arriving, but no one knows where or when. Under the threat of a Fascist reprisal, a group of men, women, and children, guided by an old man, Galvano Galvani, decides to abandon the city at night to go on a long, clandestine journey through the countryside, cutting through the olive groves, to reach safety in Sant'Angelo, a nearby town. Silently, they eat bread and leave by night. Shortly thereafter, at three in the morning, while stopping by a well they hear the explosions from their city, which is being blown up.

The journey will last three days, along dug up roads, past burnt out farm houses; at night they will stop in the most inhospitable of places and eat whatever they find. It is the story of an odyssey that will lead to the establishment of a new community. In fact, the voyage of these refugees is punctuated by symbolic encounters, like all great mythical journeys. There is the path of Mara—a Sicilian woman who, thinking she hears the Americans, runs up against a German machine-gun hidden among the bushes—which seems to represent the sirens, the destructive force of illusion. There is the little Fascist child who, protected by the presence of his father, breaks out like a small, wild fury and later, terrified at the moment of defeat, will climb up in a tree screaming and crying, searching futilely to escape death: the illusion of power. There is the passage in front of a dairy farm in flames that arouses fear in the young Cecilia, whose mother then teaches her a popular old nursery rhyme to exorcise her demons. There is the motorcade of defeated Germans who return, downcast, toward their distant homes, bringing with them a broken down bus pulled by mules, and singing Wagner's "Death of Isolde." There is the swim in the dried up lake of the Arno, which is like a new baptism, and the encounter with the partisans—another birth where all the young men who join the group of fighters change their names.

Then at the end, when everything seems resolved, tragedy arrives in the form of a clash with the Fascists, the fratricidal struggle like that between Romulus and Remus, in the myth of the foundation of Rome. While reapers are working in hills parched by the August sun, a group of Fascists arrive, patrolling the area in search of provisions. They gather some ears of corn and are about to leave when a battle erupts with the partisans. They all run, moving in all directions through the cornfield. The movie camera follows the frightened men, sliding low to the ground (again a reminder of Rossellini, of the sixth grand episode of *Paisan*). We know and see almost nothing. Some old friends meet up, greet each other as always, then suddenly remember they

Concetta bathing in
the shallows of the
river Arno, between
Florence and
San Miniato.

are enemies and shoot at each other. Some Fascists run toward a wounded man and, next to them, some partisans are taking care of another, one of their own: "Would you pass me the water?" one asks the other group, but having realized just in time that he has spoken to the enemy, he immediately shoulders his rifle, shoots and at the same time falls to the earth, dead, like the others on both sides. All dead. The Black Shirts fare worst in the battle. The young Cecilia looks on, terrified. Finally, History becomes clothed in the grandiose garments of Myth. A young, isolated Fascist runs away but doesn't succeed in escaping the fury of the people. An old man follows him with a pitchfork, just as in the fresco of the devils. And right here, in an epic blaze, we return to the Trojan War. The partisans, in Cecilia's eyes, appear dressed in ancient armor like breast-plated Achaean warriors; they all rise up together with their gilded armor and the Fascist falls amid the corn, pierced by a thousand lances. History is seen through the eyes of Myth, and Myth is reinterpreted through the eyes of History. The earth is bloodied by brothers who have killed one another, as has happened often in Italy's history.

Galvano confesses
his old love
to Concetta.

The story is over, we go back to the beginning, to the star-studded sky, and the shooting star conjoins memory with the realization of desires, historic fact with the imaginary, testimony with invention. As Mario Isnenghi has observed, in this film "everything gushes fresh, unprecedented, extraordinary, with the taste of adventure (which is extremely strong in this film), of the unrepeatable" . . . but at the same time "everything is codified, subject to rules: the *Iliad* and melodrama. It is no accident that the characters say and explicate that they have the impression of living lives already lived."

This films recounts the symbolic birth of a new community, it tells of a regenerative dream that man has always carried within him. Even the first image, in the mother's story, is one of a detachment, a birth. In the midst of the Tuscan countryside, beneath the sun, ripe fruit falls off a tree and rolls to the ground, while Corrado, the protagonist, emerges from the earth and climbs up into the daylight. The earth also finds a symbol, a constant metaphorical image, in the matronly Signora Concetta, who follows the group of poor refugees. In her youth, Concetta was loved by Galvano, but secretly, since poverty made it impossible for him to aspire to the hand of a lady. Now Concetta the old woman has become a sort of archaic, Demeter-like divinity. The Taviani's religious feeling is pre-Christian. It is a religious feeling for the earth, the landscape, Tuscany, the world. Concetta, who for the entire journey remains silent as an idol, will speak to Galvano, hero-founder of the new community, only at the end. She will spend one night with him, as in every great myth that is worthy of respect, even if here the two heroes are elderly. But she is also a signora, from the wealthy, landowning class. Along the entire journey she undergoes a process of shedding, as she becomes deprived of all her jewels, which she gives to the girl child. She even abandons her hat, her coat, her stockings, all her glitter, until she is reduced to pure body, like one of those statuettes of Mediterranean mothers, symbols of fecundity in the second millenium BC.

This grand divinity that Galvano carries along with him is also his destination, his point of arrival: marrying her, he marries Mother Earth, and from her he reacquires the strength to establish a new society. The church of the explosion, which in the film is the duomo of San Martino, and in reality is the collegiate church of Arezzo, is, instead, the place where the grand nightmare of History unfolds, with Troy in flames, devastated, from which the shipwrecked survivors depart. San Martino (San Miniato) is the land of real time, where History passes with its weight of destruction, death, and chaos. Sant'Angelo, in the end, seen from below, at the mountain's summit, is the land where History does not arrive, and where the mythical cycle begins again. Traditionally, in all myths, the mountain represents the center of the world, the place where the sky is closest to the earth. During the night the community always

The liberating rain at the end of the story.

Fiorile. **The square of Villa Saletta, a place of used in the Tavianis' films.**

finds itself in circular places, like sacred sites: the well, the volcanic bomb crater. And the encounter between the young Cecilia and the Americans takes place in the midst of an olive grove, an Edenic site, symbol of Tuscany and the entire world: the world as it should be or as it could be, life as a game, an encounter between two young foreigners and a child, who communicate by making faces in the meadow, next to a cross.

TUSCANY AS SPACE-TIME

Time constricts, the centuries interweave in an inextricable knot over this timeless landscape. We are in *Fiorile*. A French car travels through the night. Inside are a man, a woman, and two sleeping children. Dawn can be glimpsed far off on the horizon and the boy asks, "What is that light down there?" "It is Tuscany" the father answers, indicating his deep love for his native land. This is the beginning of *Fiorile*, a Jacobin name for the month of April. This time, the Taviani brothers recount the legend of a peasant family grown rich from a box of gold stolen from Napoleon's troops. A young lieutenant, Jean, was guarding his regiment's strongbox, but was distracted by his love for a peasant girl, Elisabetta. Meanwhile, without her knowing, her brother Corrado steals the gold and hides it at home. It is an impoverished farmstead, inhabited by honest people without a scrap of bread. His father curses him, the entire family curses him, but Corrado wants to become rich at all costs. The blond-haired Jean, the young soldier who allowed himself to be robbed, is left alone one night in the town piazza and at dawn is shot in a clearing at the top of a windy hill, while poor Elisabetta, in love with Jean, runs desperately through the fields covered with cornflowers and collapses atop large

clusters of lavender. A long racking shot pulls away from them and returns to the present. The story seems to run along with the car, while the father recites the old legend to his children. Time passes, and the Benedetti family becomes rich, but the gold weighs on the family like a nightmare, and the "Benedetti" ("blessed ones" in Italian), come to be known as the "Maledetti" ("the damned"). The film tells of their subsequent fortunes and misadventures, crimes and impossible loves, violence and vendettas. Two centuries unfold before us: the nineteenth and the twentieth. The father's story to his children continues with an episode that recalls the Boccaccio-like tale of Lisabetta and her two cruel brothers who assassinate the young manservant with whom she is in love. It is 1903. Elisa and Alessandro, two children in the family, give a grand reception to celebrate Alessandro's election to parliament. But Elisa hates her brother. She is in love with a young peasant, and like Elisabetta, she too has suffered the unexpected disappearance of her beloved. For Alessandro, deeming this love unseemly for his political career, has forced the poor young man to leave for Australia. Like Elisabetta before her, Elisa begins to harbor the same hatred in her heart for her brother. She accompanies her brothers on a trip to the countryside and during a picnic poisons them with mushrooms. Here the landscape—the same one where Boccaccio set his tale—seems to be a participant in the story. Added to the mystery of nature is the mystery of the relationships between man and woman, between brother and sister. But the dark legends are now over, the journey of the young French family has neared its end. Now, we see Massimo, the last of the Benedetti, in the farmhouse, which has returned to its initial impoverished state. He has taken the curse upon himself, accepting condemnation, expiation, and solitude. The children are dubious and perplexed: is this a legend or a true story? The elderly Massimo is the grandfather of the children we have seen en route. He is a somewhat eccentric type who has given away all his worldly goods. The clues accumulate, the mystery grows more dense. In the attic of the old Benedetti farmhouse there is a puppet of a French soldier and the old man prepares some mushrooms he has gathered in the meadows for dinner. The children, having grown frightened, do not want to eat them, but their grandfather insists: they are all legends. And yet, who knows, perhaps there is something… During the return trip in the car, the boy grasps in his hand a coin he found in the attic, a gold napoleon.

Legends are never only legends. The La Petraia villa, the Frescobaldi farm, the Villa Saletta Forcoli estate are all famous names on the agendas of foreign tourists, but here these places, where *Fiorile* was shot, recapture all their mystery.

THE DANGEROUS ALCHEMY OF NATURE

This mysterious Tuscany, mother and land unknown even to its own inhabitants, is the protagonist of another film, *Elective Affinities*, an adaptation of Goethe's novel. The Taviani have transposed the story to Tuscany, recreating the same atmosphere as those of the original's romantic scenes.

Once again we are in the past, but a past that is completely like our own time. Even if the characters wear nineteenth century clothing, the Tuscan landscape always remains the same, ancient and new, present and distant. As it presents itself to our eyes, it also seems to elude us, closed off in the distant depths of its horizons. Edoardo and Carlotta have lost possession of their estate and are proposing to turn it into a modern park. Edoardo would like to invite a friend and share with him the happiness he is experiencing. Carlotta has a vague presentiment and would like to remain alone with her husband in the beautiful Tuscan landscape.

Here the character of the Captain has become an architect, who plans a magnificent romantic garden, with groves, pathways, a lake, and sloping meadows. One evening, during the habitual reading with which the three friends end their day, the architect explains the meaning of elective affinities, the turbid game of nature that always shifts and recombines its elements according to new attractions. If A and B are close, the intervention of a third element, C, could draw one of these and thus break the closeness of the first two. This is what now happens to Carlotta, who feels alone, while Edoardo spends his days measuring the terrain with his friend and with a new magnificent tool the architect has brought, a theodolite, which finally allows him to know the surfaces, slopes, and

Elective Affinities.
The color of passion: Carlotta (Isabelle Huppert) in the rose-garden.

Carlotta, Edoardo,
Ottilia at the party
on the lake.

shapes of the hills. However another element arrives, Ottilia, to attempt to re-establish the earlier equilibrium. Carlotta invites her niece, hoping that she will provide companionship during her long, solitary days. But nature shifts its elements according to different and often cruel games. Ottilia and Edoardo fall in love, which is what happens to Carlotta and the architect as well. The story, which concludes with the death of Edoardo and Ottilia, tells of the power of nature over creatures that believe they can dominate it. And the theodolite, that magnificent invention, beneath which the Tuscan hills are transformed into a garden, reveals its impotence to control the much vaster landscape of the soul.

Goethe's story seems somewhat diminished in the Taviani's over-refined and sober staging, but the landscape helps them, with its proud and archaic beauty, as always, to overcome the difficulties of staging so grand a tale—one of the most profound works in Western literature.

In the Taviani's films, the beauty of the Tuscan landscape is always so mysterious and contradictory. Cruel in its indifference and in its millennial distance, it seems, at other times, to participate in our deepest emotions, to want to ease our tormented souls with sweetness and serenity, or instead to disturb even the most placid among us. It is a "non-indifferent nature," to use the phrase of another master, the great father of cinema, Sergei Eisenstein, who has never ceased being an inspiration to the Taviani.

STEFANO SOCCI

KAOS AND TU RIDI: THE TAVIANIS INTERPRET PIRANDELLO

To understand how the Taviani brothers look at Pirandello, we need to dwell a moment on that "old ingenuous and mannered print" in *Short Stories for a Year* (written over a long period of time and brought together as a collection in 1922). There, the author analyzes the print down to its smallest compositional detail and describes it both as pictorial space and as a stage set. Pirandello's well-known negative opinion of sound-film was voiced in his essay "*Se il film parlante abolirà il teatro*" ("If talking films will abolish theater," 1929). There he states that, "the voice is a living body that emits, and in film we don't have the bodies of actors, as in theater, but their images photographed in movement." He goes on to say that, "the images don't speak: one merely sees them; if they speak, the living voice is in implacable contrast with their quality of

shadows and crowding, like an unnatural thing that discovers and denounces a mechanism." The voice that resounds in the movie hall has an "extremely disagreeable" effect "of unreality"; due to the foreground of speaking images, the "scenic framework is lost." "In this way," Pirandello adds, "perfection will not be able to lead the filmmaker to abolish theater, but, possibly, to abolish himself. Theater will stay original, ever-living, and from time to time mutable, like every other living thing." Cinema, instead, "will be its one-time copy, stereotyped, fundamentally all the more illogical and unnatural, the more it attempts to draw near its original, to the point of replacing it."

Given this prejudice, the setting for *Looking at a Print*—a path lined by gigantic eucalyptus trees, to the left, a knoll where we can make out a nocturnal shelter, at the foot of the knoll a container into which water is running—comes alive thanks to the mastery of the playwright. Two beggars are chatting as they walk along the path; a short way behind them they have left a knapsack and a crutch. The play of light and shadows allows one to discern that it is a moonlit dawn. At the end, when the conversation between the beggars once again turns to the subject of women, the writer hurriedly suspends the action: "(Perhaps it is best to end here. It's not worth it to linger to waste our imagination on this old, mannered print)."

One could say that this is precisely how the Taviani brothers begin to approach Pirandello, from the meager and precious suggestions that surface in the short story and in the essay. First of all there is the silence. The author contemplates the yellowed engraving, imagining that the only noises in that tenuous but ample moonlight are the chirping of a cricket, the soft flow of the water and the rustling of the foliage of the trees, while from far away there arrives the "stifled roar" of small town life. The magical, silent night, and the sacred voices of nature are opposed to the invasive and annoying sounds of the town. The sublime landscape picture—later complicated by a pre-Beckettian development (Pirandello's beggars

are similar to those in *Waiting for Godot*)—suffers the shame of the mechanical world, of a disgraced word on a level with a "coarse grumbling by ventriloquists, accompanied by that intolerable drone and sputtering of gramophones," as the author underlines in regard to sound-film in the essay mentioned earlier. If cinema is the symbol and expression of the century of technological growth, of an existence corrupted by mass production, how can the Tavianis reappropriate Pirandello's theatrical naturalism—that *lost scenic framework*, that eloquent, dominant silence that—suggested by the wonderful descriptions of the geographic and human landscape of Sicily, substantiates, even more than the dialogue, the plot of *Short Stores for a Year*?

In the films the two Tuscan brothers have dedicated to Pirandello, *Kaos* (1984) and *Tu ridi* (1998), adapted more or less freely from *Short Stories for a Year*, one thing is certain: people always are equivalent to nature. Rural culture, tormented and oppressed, represented by its more humble and anonymous heroes, clashes, on the harsh battlefield of rocks and sunny plains, with the champions of the dominant, landowning, urban, and predominantly bourgeois culture. In *Kaos*, the importance and sacred nature of the *silent landscape* are immediately made evident by the overhead flight of a crow and by the fairy-tale-like tolling of the bell it wears at its neck. In the short story *The Crow of Mizzaro*, some loafing shepherds have captured and tortured a crow and finally reward it with a little bronze bell. Like a sad clown (the bird, male, was surprised brooding over eggs, like a female), the crow in the film flies over Sicily, reclaiming the scenic shot and, at the same time, distancing itself from the world on its thread of silence. Suffering, solitude, and disorientation are characteristics of human nature, which, in the play of oppositions offered by Pirandello, this time struggle against original brutishness, freed from harrowing psychological complications. These characteristics are stressed by a caption superimposed against the aerial evolutions of the crow: "… I, then, am the son of Chaos, and not allegorically, but truly, in reality, because I was born in our countryside, found near a dense forest called *Càvusu* by the inhabitants of Girgenti: a dialectical corruption of the true, ancient Greek word *Kàos*."

Pirandello deems the Siculian ethnos to be the "corrupt" legacy of classical Greece, and so the lost scenic framework that the Tavianis must rediscover takes on the outlines, tones, and types of an epic tradition. The first episode of *Kaos*, entitled *The Other Son* and inspired by a homonymous short story, is set literally in a desolate, archaic landscape. In the shot of a plateau parched by the son, a road is wedged in, flanked by low stone walls, traveled by a group of emigrants, made sorrowful by the presence of an elderly woman in mourning, Maragrazia. This is one version, more harsh and concise, of the *tableau vivant* of *Looking at a Print*. The protagonist wants to give one of the travelers, en route to America, a letter for her two sons who live in Santa Fe and have been away for some fourteen years. A doctor in the group notices a taciturn man who never loses sight of Maragrazia and places food for her on the wall. It is the third son, "decent, respectful, honest," but the mother keeps him at a distance and fears him. She tells the doctor how she conceived him, and the dusty print comes alive with passion in a flashback. Garibaldi, arriving on the island with a thousand red-shirted soldiers, opens the gates of the prisons and ferocious assassins, now set free, roam the countryside. One day Maragrazia's husband, who fails to return from working in the fields. She goes looking for him, comes upon the brigands of Cola Camizzi in their lair, as they play at bocce with the

Kaos. **The damned and disowned son.**

head of their unfortunate victim. She is spared but taken by force by the lieutenant, Trupía, who is the father of Rocco, the son she rejects. The landscape resurrects the stony horizons of Hellas, and the mother, a shadowy and solitary hired mourner, evokes the specter of Jocasta. If Rocco Trupía is none other than Oedipus, the interpretation of Maragrazia also refers to classical tragedy, sent as she is from the "land of weeping" to the "beautiful land of gold."

The mythological, anthropological, and social dimension—closely linked by the Tavianis to the Mediterranean landscape, to ancient agrarian cults and to fertility rites—is exemplified by their frequent recurrence to the brilliance of the crops, indeed to the "beautiful land of gold," soon bloodied and violated by an awareness of death, or the "land of weeping." The sacrifice is a prelude to birth, as in the Greek myth of Persephone. The sequence of the battle in the field of ripened corn, the most effective image in *Night of the Shooting Stars* (1982) is emblematic for all these scenes. In the summer of 1944, in Tuscany, women and partisans are intent on the harvest and are surprised by the Fascists, people like them; former friends and acquaintances. The clash, without quarter or pity, is suddenly "frozen" by a hallucination of the little girl who, now a woman, tells the entire story in the long flashback that is the film. The young protagonist before the corn field behaves like Pirandello before the yellowed engraving. Atrocity and violence, located in a remote and indifferent natural setting, once erased by the poetic imagination, reclaim the extraordinary, eternal symbolic vigor of myth. From the platinum ears of corn there arise, literally generated by the earth, a band of warriors in shining armor, sporting ancient-style helmets and lances. Hurled in unison, these pierce what, for the young girl, is the representation of evil, a Fascist who has just shot at an elderly and unarmed man. Frozen in a scenic shot—beyond the curtain of appearances and objectivity—flow the individual reality and the subjective schemes, for which the myth is the interpretive key.

The same thing happens in the second episode of *Kaos*, inspired by the short story *Moon Blindness*. Batà and Sidora, who have been married for twenty years, have settled into an old, isolated house. As Pirandello writes, "amidst the desert of that stubble, without a tree around, without a scrap of shade." There is no theater or screen better than this, for the Tavianis. According to the Greeks, the moon was a goddess, the disturbing Selene on her chariot of silver. If the sun represented Apollo and the virile luminosity of power, the nocturnal body suggested the languors, the malice, and the mysteries of a female universe. Moonlight is not congenial to man, because it puts him in touch with his most secret and disturbing aspect. As a child, Batà's mother carelessly left him exposed to the moon's beams and, since that time, has been fascinated by the goddess. When the moon gleams, white and round in the sky, the protagonist orders his wife to lock herself in the house and to not open the door, even if he is outside, moaning, screaming, and tortured in the feral ecstasies of werewolfism. In *Looking at a Print* Pirandello also attributes a disquieting quality to moonlight. Amid a stage-set of the absurd, the moon shines down on two squalid beggars, the overbearing Rosso and the pale Alfreduccio, a frail and "fawning" blind man who has never had a woman. The other, more experienced man, teaches him that the blind have good luck with the fairer sex, because "the woman, understand? Everything's there that she needs for doing it without her being seen." This echoes the phrase used by Marco, the

Zì Dima and
Don Lollò in the
episode *The Jar*.

mendicant blind soothsayer: "All blind! All blind!" In *Moon Blindness* Sidora, regretting that she has married Batà for his money, invites her mother and her former lover, Saro, to keep her company in her farmhouse when her husband is in the throes of his illness. She taunts, seduces, and flirts with Saro. The clouds cover the moon and Batà sees the lovers in bed: that moment's break from the enchantment that blinds him allows him to perceive a heretofore unseen glimpse of femininity. Pirandello is not tender with women and thus nor are the Tavianis in their Pirandellian works.

In the third episode, *The Jar*, the off screen voice of Pirandello (Omero Antonutti) accompanies the cart that brings the vessel, "large as an abbess," destined to hold the new oil to the Promosole farmstead, the center of the vast estate belonging to Don Lollò Zirafa. In the story everything revolves around the symbolic values of the sacred golden fluid, which pagan athletes used to sprinkle upon themselves and with which, in the Christian world, the dead are anointed to allow them access to the beyond. In *The Jar*, however, the oil is not shown. The gigantic terracotta amphora, placed at the center of the inner courtyard, on a square pedestal that

resembles a model of an Aztec temple, is not fated to be filled with the essence of olives. That night, abetted by the full moon, the container splits in half. They call in Zi' Dima Licasi, a man who repairs broken vessels, and on the large stone floor, blazing with heat, he introduces a note of shadow and threatening imperfection. He is hunchbacked, wrapped in a black cloak, and it is said that he uses a prodigious adhesive and is renowned as a sorcerer. Don Lollò demands that in addition to using the adhesive, the craftsman repair the crack with iron staples. Zi' Dima is offended but carries out the task and, working inside the jar, realizes that once it has been repaired, his hump will prevent him from exiting. Here we are witnesses to an inversion of the symbolic values delineated in the first part of the story. The enormous jar, symbol of Don Lollò's wealth and diurnal, solar, Christian power over bodies and things has been shattered by lunar witchcraft. The presumption and arrogance of the landowner are humbled by the world of magic, championed by Zi' Dima, a man of the people. Day must necessarily give way to night. Having re-established the *natural* equilibrium, which was compromised by Don Lollò's sin of hubris, the celestial divinities and the lesser gods—landlords and servants—can carry on a dialogue. Don Lollò doesn't want the Zi' Dima to break the repaired urn in order to free himself. A lawyer reminds him that this is tantamount to kidnapping, but it is not reason or legalities that will justly resolve the dispute. So, at the end of the landowner's day, the congenial darkness always falls on Zi' Dima, and the latter organizes, beneath the moon, a celebration in which Don Lollò's hired help participate. Men and women dance in a circle around the jar, which—given the inverted ceremony, the subversion of the diurnal order— does not contain oil. It no longer represents the owner, but becomes a pagan altar, a stage for Satan, the immobile force behind the illuminated circus of Selene's rays, symbol of the revenge of ancient cults oppressed by a single religion, by a single truth. The Sabbath is interrupted abruptly; Don Lollò strikes the jar, which rolls over and breaks once again into pieces. Zi' Dima has won and is carried away in triumph.

The figure of the square, which in *The Jar* expresses the reason-power union, is opposed to the geometry of the circle, or the fluid and eternally mutable space of the esoteric-natural dimension, what anthropologists call the meta-historic horizon. In the short story and the film,

the most interesting idea is the significant hiding of the oil. This strong presence *in absentia* allows Pirandello to tie, as antagonists, the ancient world and modern society. And it allows the Tavianis to develop their usual reflection on the essence of power. The large square of the farmhouse courtyard imprisons the circle of the proletarian dancers who, in their turn, enclose the square pedestal (with chutes that, seen form above, form a cross), within which another circle, that of the jar, dominates. It is as if they are saying that the conflict is eternal and inexorable, or rather a constituent part of human nature. Yet the oil provides color to the landscape, so that Don Lollò's dwelling place and the olive groves, bathed in golden light, suggest the ubiquitous extension of natural or Christian spirituality. Gold always has been the color of power and divinity, but in Medieval painting, if one scrapes away the flakes of gold background, what comes to the surface is a thin layer of clay that allows the gilding to adhere over time. Beneath the gold, at the base of the gods, and at the root of the myth, there is always fragile and perishable mortal substance.

In the fourth episode, *Requiem*, a transcription of the short story *Requiem aeternam dona eis, Domine!*, some peasants and shepherds on the

Màrgari estate to into town to ask the baron for permission to make themselves a cemetery. The off screen voice of Pirandello punctuates the phases of the confrontation between the closed urban square, symbol of order and "civilization," and the hairy, Dionysian inhabitants of the countryside. The latter have uncombed beards and wear cow skins, and the baron, indignant and frightened, orders the police to accompany the men back to the farm, where the elderly tribal patriarch waits for his relatives to finish digging his grave. The police begin to destroy the improvised cemetery but they stop before the false death of the old man who, later, "rises again," affirming his ethnic right—his close relationship with the earth upon which his group has lived for generations. This is a question of implicit natural ownership, conferred by work and suffering, which precedes and transcends any "legal" right exercised by the baron. If the populace is nature, nature always is seen in opposition to bourgeois civilization.

The epilogue, entitled *Conversation with my Mother*, imagines that Luigi Pirandello, now white-haired and this time shown to us in the flesh, returns to Sicily for the first time since the death of his mother. The "son of Chaos" reclaims the earth that gave birth to him and that is already ready to take him back (like the earth that awaits the venerable old man in the previous episode). At the station of his native village he finds his old friend Saro, Sidora's lover in *Moon Blindness*, who accompanies him in a gig. They stop by; the ruins of a Greek theater. At home the protagonist converses with the ghost of his mother. The woman, a deified icon, advises him to learn to see things through the eyes of one who is no longer alive, and this will make him "more sacred and more beautiful." She then tells him of a sea voyage, toward Malta, she made with her family. They have to reach their father who, after the revolution of 1848, is being persecuted by the Bourbons, and they stop for a few hours on the pumice-stone islet. The mother, a young girl, keeps Pirandello's grandmother company, while her brothers and sisters run free on the dazzling slopes. The little girl cries at being left out, although she didn't want to join in the games.

Here an element emerges that defines the Taviani's Pirandellian interpretation, namely, how melancholy is connected to a precocious, structural and biographical aging and pain. *Kaos* is a mirror that reflects the crisis of the early nineteenth century, the same senility that strikes

Svevo, Joyce's, and Thomas Mann's heroes. In all the episodes, the symbology of death triumphs. It is seen as a geographic-affective distancing (*The Other Son*), unshakable solitude (*Moon Blindness*), the defeat of natural forms of worship, despite their ephemeral revenge (*The Jar*), the proud agony of patriarchal society (*Requiem*), and the mournful story-telling of shades (*Conversation with My Mother*). The decline due to the passage of years is placed on the same pathological level as the enchantment that afflicts the young Batà. Death is surely the most fatal virus but some suffer it too soon, at a tender age, and don't succeed in living without a sense of death, so that existence becomes equal to an illness.

If the yellowed print provides Pirandello the occasion for the setting of an action, a scenic framework, in Pirandello-like fashion *Kaos*, precisely as a sound-film that is spoken, denounces the irrecoverable loss of the original picture, of the life and truth of theater that come to light only – as in a swan song – in the wild nocturnal dance of *The Jar*.

* * *

Tu ridi, the other Taviani film inspired by Pirandello, was conceived originally in three episodes. The writer appeared in the first episode, a long prologue entitled *The Daughter*, set in 1934, on the day it was announced that Pirandello had won the Nobel Prize. Joy at well-deserved recognition is obfuscated by nostalgia for his daughter Lietta, the unhappy wife of a Chilean diplomat. Pirandello recalls the first staging of *Six Characters in Search of an Author*, at the Teatro Valle in Rome, the tumultuous public reception; Lietta's proud defense of his work in the face of his detractors' whistles. After shooting this episode, using Pirandello's actual studio, The Tavianis decided to cut it out, on the eve of the 1998 Venice Film Festival. Perhaps they had the same questions about its length, etc. that, earlier, had pushed them to the *Requiem* episode from *Kaos*, restoring it only in the television version.

Only a slim bit of the prologue remains, consisting of the protagonist's off screen voice, that introduces the first episode, *Felice*, taken form the short story *Tu ridi*. Felice Tespini, a promising baritone who had to give up his career because of illness, and has becomea book-keeper at the Teatro dell'Opera, is often discovered laughing in his sleep by his Bulgarian wife, Marika. The doctor says that the "disturbance" is the result of pleasant dreams. "In life," he adds, "one would like to do

one thing and finds oneself doing something else." The theme is identical to the thread that runs through the novel *The Late Mattia Pascal* (1904). It is no accident that the first edition of the essay *Humor* (1908) is dedicated to this famous personality: "to the dear departed Mattia Pascal, librarian." In the essay, Pirandello quotes the philosophers of the idealistic and romantic German post-Kantian movement: "The ego, the only true reality, Hegel explained, can smile at the vain appearance of the universe; as it accepts it, it can also annul it; it cannot take its own creation seriously. Thence irony: namely that force— according to Ludwig Tieck—that allows the poet to dominate the material he deals with; material that is reduced—according to Frederick Schlegel— to a perpetual parody, to a transcendental farce."

Humor, which for Pirandello is equivalent to a "contrary feeling," is manifest in *Felice* with an overturning that is also a compensation. The protagonist laughs at night because during the day he has no reason to do so. The shadows are a space consecrated to freedom, a moment when the individual reappropriates his "only true reality." In *The Jar* the humor emerges in the same manner, deriding and overturning the diurnal power, in the form of obscure clowning. Those

Facing page: The actor Omero Antonutti playing Luigi Pirandello.

who are oppressed by the light find consolation and a dwelling place beneath the mantle of Selene. The contemplation of night prefigures illness and death. The lovers of the moon, such as Batà and Zi' Dima in *Kaos*, are considered monsters when we see them in full daylight. Felice Tespini is also "different," since he is in hiding from existence, affected by the same illness as Mattia Pascal. Bent over the master ledger, he is not devoted to the double entry, but prefers to dream about what has been and can no longer be. He lives in exile from himself and this laceration—this detachment from others, the diurnal elements: Rome of the Fascist period, his tart wife, the authoritarian theater director, Gino Migliori—lead him gloomily toward suicide. Not before the

Tu ridi.
The cruel joke of the fascists and Felice's laugh "buried" in the dream.

Tavianis have time to emphasize the meaning of an event taken directly from the novel, however, Felice dreams that his colleague Tobia Rambaldi, a meek and grayish man with a limp, is mocked by two of the director's thugs while he climbs a staircase. They cause him to fall, taking away his walking stick, which they then use to pierce his behind. This macabre "transcendental farce," which stages the spectacle of Felice's and Tobia's daily frustrations in the world of dreams, finds its natural conclusion in the death of the two friends. Tobia precedes his friend to the beyond, taking an overdose of sleeping pills. Felice follows the director home, threatens him with a toy pistol and forces him to admit he is an imbecile. However, the Pirandellian humor reserves to the protagonist a final, sorrowful occasion to avenge his destiny. Arriving at the sea, the book-keeper prepares to take his final swim but, in an irony of fate, just when he seems cheered at the prospect of drowning—having decided to return to the prenatal womb—there appears on the beach a young singer, Nora. They had worked together and he also had been somewhat in love with her. The girl is there to perform at a holiday arena, and she invites him to lunch, smiles at him, sweetly ogles him, and convinces him to perform again before her table companions, his "war-horse," the finale to the second act of Rossini's *Italiana in Algeri*. Felice the clown sings again, and relives a moment from his past. He receives applause and then Nora distances herself, charmed by a man in the orchestra. The sad clown hurries through his

"nasty affair," acting out the farewell scene at the water's edge: his hat, jacket, and a letter he had slipped into his pocket are all that remain of him.

In the second episode, *Two Kidnappings,* taken from the short *story The Capture*, we are once again in Sicily. The only guests in a mountain hotel are Vincenzo, son of the stool-pigeon, Sebastiano Cangemi, and Rocco, the Mafioso who is guarding him. From the terrace one can glimpse Mount Ballarò, where, as the kidnapper relates, one hundred years before, a respected old doctor was held hostage. In a flashback the old man and his custodians are fraternizing. The man knows that his relatives will not pay the ransom because it is in all their interests that he dies. In *Kaos* the individuals tied to the countryside, instinctive and animal-like but in harmony with the forces of nature, don't succeed in carrying on a dialogue with the representatives of the gloomy urban and bourgeois domain. Fourteen years after their first Pirandellian film, the Tavianis have managed to reconcile, in *Two Kidnappings*, the motives of both sides. The old man resists this miserable prison, a shepherd's hut, but then adapts and begins to communicate with the "young men." He tells them about the speed of light, about Galileo, and the rotation of the earth, he teaches them that "things are not only how you are accustomed to seeing them, but also how you want to see them." The directors transform him into an archaic, venerable character, into a Greek philosopher. If Ballarò gives the natives the fire of knowledge and civilization, they give him an ascetic life, far from secular anxieties, and a serene death, surrounded by the affection of a small rural community. The composition of tensions that run back and forth between the anthropological and ideological polarities is relegated, however, to the past, to the enchanted mountain. A century later, someone has brought a newspaper into the isolated hotel, where they read that the stool-pigeon Cangemi has begun to collaborate with the State. The Mafia, symbol of a territory and psyche not yet colonized by governmental order, commands that Rocco kill the boy. The execution has the nature of a ritual sacrifice, where classical, pagan justice is manifested. Rocco picks up a large stone and brings it down again and again on Vincenzo's head, before dumping the boy in a vat of acid. The final images show us the murderer intent on a dance that resembles a liberating Bacchic ecstasy, even though he is behind the bars of a cell.

In the essay *Humor*, Pirandello quotes Socrates: "One is the origin of joy and sadness; in contrapositions, an idea is only recognized by its opposite; comedy and tragedy are made from the same material." *Tu ridi* seems to illustrate this fundamental axiom. The mask of comedy is flanked by its dramatic rival; mediated by the sentimental contribution of the narrator (the off screen voice). Both lead the spectator to the sole matrix of comedy and tragedy—life. If we compare the more recent Pirandellian film to *Kaos*, which had greater critical and public success, curiously, it turns out that it is *Tu ridi* that has the more solid and coherent structure. The author's smile is never severed from sorrow, or rather in Pirandello's post-romantic picture, tears and melancholy humor balance out the obvious humanity of the laugh. In *Tu ridi* the Tavianis collect two extreme examples, because it is the very sensibility of the writer that requires a dual and conflicting scheme. But the narrative fragmentation of *Kaos*, the plurality of its suggestions, distracts from the crude struggle between the two halves of existence that still underlie the folkloric appearance of the film. "The artist must sense his own work as he senses himself and he must will it as he wills himself," Pirandello explains. "Having an end and an external will means withdrawing from art."

FILMOGRAPHY

by Lucia Cardone

SHORT FILMS

1954
San Miniato, july '44 (San Miniato, luglio '44)
Treatment and direction: Valentino Orsini, Paolo and Vittorio Taviani – *Consulting, commentary and screenplay:* Cesare Zavattini – *Photography:* Renato Carmassi – *Music:* Mario Zafred.

1954 – 1959
Curtatone and Montanara (Curtatone e Montanara)
Carlo Pisacane
Painters in the City (Pittori in città)
Villas of Brianza (Villa della Brianza)
Volterra, Medieval City (Volterra, città medievale)
Stoneworkers (Lavoratori della pietra)
Sunday Madmen (I pazzi della domenica)
Carvunara
Alberto Moravia
Treatment, screenplay and direction: Valentino Orsini, Paolo and Vittorio Taviani

1960
Italy is Not a Poor Country (L'Italia non è un paese povero)
Treatment, screenplay and direction: Joris Ivens, Paolo and Vittorio Taviani – *Commentary:* Alberto Moravia, Corrado Sofia – *Voiceover:* Enrico Maria Salerno – *Photography:* Mario Dolci, Oberdan Trojani, Marco Volpi – *Music:* Gino Marinuzzi – *Editing:* Joris Ivens, Mario Rosada

FEATURES

A MAN FOR BURNING (Un uomo da bruciare, 1962)

production: Giuliani G. De Negri and Henryck Chroscicki for Ager Film / Sancro Film / Alfa Cinematografica;

direction: Valentino Orsini, Paolo and Vittorio Taviani; *treatment and screenplay:* Valentino Orsini, Paolo and Vittorio Taviani; *photography:* Toni Secchi; *set design:* Piero Poletto; *editing:* Lionello Massobrio; *music:* Gianfranco Intra; *actors:* Gian Maria Volonté, Didi Perego, Spyros Fokas, Lidia Alfonsi, Marina Malfatti, Vittorio Duse, Alessandro Sperlì, Marcella Rovena, Gianpaolo Serra, Alfonso D'Errico, Turi Ferro; *distribution:* Cino Del Duca; *running time:* 92 minutes; black and white.

After a long stay on the mainland, Salvatore Carnevale returns to his native town in Sicily with grand hopes and plans. Within a month he has decided to incite the farm workers to occupy their lands, however, the peasants get there before him and set the occupation for the following day.

Salvatore pushes them to go further—to force the Mafiosi landowners to respect agrarian reform, the land must be ploughed and planted, precisely as if the peasants were themselves the landowners. The proceedings are interrupted by an assault by men from the Mafia, but intervention by the police avoids bloodshed thereby signaling an important victory for the farm workers as well as for Salvatore. Nonetheless, at the Congress of the League of Farmers he is opposed and outvoted by his fellow workers who are tired of his too radical and personality-driven attitude.

Fear of being rejected by his people throws Salvatore into a crisis so profound that he is driven to feign illness in order to obtain comfort and consolation from Barbara, his former lover. In fact, it will be the Mafia that restores him to a prominent role among his comrades. As more profitable interests have taken over on the large estate—in the form of government orders for the construction of new roads—the gentlemen must make the workers labor for twelve hours a day to ensure that they obtain the

A Man for Burning. The mafia member and, in the background, Salvatore.

contract and, consequently, they try to buy Salvatore, hiring him as a foreman so that he can keep the workers under control. At first he pretends to accept—taking advantage of the situation to take petty revenge for the harm caused by those who had made him an outcast—but, before long, he openly challenges the Mafiosi by urging the workers to struggle for a reduction in hours.

When Salvatore is killed in an ambush, his coffin, covered with flags, is carried on the shoulders of his comrades throughout the town and beneath the windows of the Mafia bosses.

MARRIAGE OUTLAWS (I fuorilegge del matrimonio, 1963)

production: Giuliani G. De Negri, for Ager Film / film Coop / D'Errico Film; *direction:* Valentino Orsini, Paolo and Vittorio Taviani; *treatment and screenplay:* Lucio Battistrada, Renato Niccolai, Giuliani G. De Negri, Valentino Orsini, Paolo and Vittorio Taviani; *photography:* Enrico Menczer; *set design:* Lina Nerli Taviani; *editing:* Lionello Massobrio; *music:* Giovanni Fusco; *actors:* Ugo Tognazzi, Annie Girardot, Romolo Valli, Marina Malfatti, Scilla Gabel, Isa Crescenzi, Didi Perego; *distribution:* Cidif; *running time:* 100 minutes; black and white.

The film addresses the theme of divorce. In fact, in 1963 Italy the Sansone law was being debated. Known as the "small divorce law," it attempted to introduce—at least in certain specific situations—the possibility of dissolving a marriage. *Marriage Outlaws* emerges as a sort of illustration of the drafting of this law, with five episodes and a prologue each demonstrating an exemplary case where the legislation in force impeded the dissolution of a union, despite the obvious absence of any bond between the two spouses.

The prologue unfolds in a psychiatric hospital and tells the story of a mentally ill woman, without hope of a cure, who cannot recognize her husband and believes that she is married to the clinic doctor.

The first episode tells the story of Wilma, a young woman who, married to a man condemned to life imprisonment, has a relationship with someone else. Wilma is abducted by her brother-in-law, who wants to avenge the honor of his betrayed brother and exhibits her naked on a tower.

The sad tale of Margherita and Francesco follows. Earlier marriages force them to have a clandestine relationship, even though they both have been separated from their spouses for many years. Worn down by continuous subterfuges, they break things off definitively for banal reasons of distance created by their work situation.

Giulia is the protagonist of the third episode. Years before, her husband had tried to kill her but the woman has succeeded in overcoming that terrible period and building a new family. After the passage of much time, however, her husband begins to persecute her.

The ups and downs of Vasco Timballo, an Italian emigrant, are at the center of the fourth interlude. After living and working in Africa for twenty years, Vasco—

Marriage Outlaws: women imprisoned. Below: A woman humiliated by the chastity belt.

believing his wife has died—returns to Italy to remarry. Arriving in his hometown, he discovers that his first wife isn't dead at all, as his relatives had led him to believe. The woman has chosen to become a cloistered nun and lives in a convent where Vasco cannot even enter. Despite this, the two remain tied by their matrimonial bond.

The final episode tells the story of Caterina who became a war bride at the age of fifteen by marrying an American soldier. When her husband returned to the United States, he obtained a divorce and remarried, while she remains unable to obtain an annulment from the Sacred Rota.

SUBVERSIVES (I sovversivi, 1967)

production: Giuliani G. De Negri for Ager Film; *direction:* Paolo and Vittorio Taviani; *treatment and screenplay:* Paolo and Vittorio Taviani; *photography:* Gianni Narzisi, Giuseppe Ruzzolino; *set design:* Luciano Pinelli; *costumes:* Lina Nerli Taviani; *editing:* Franco Taviani; *music:* Gianni Fusco; *actors:* Giorgio Arlorio, Giulio Brogi, Pier Paolo Capponi, Marija Tocinoswky, Lucio Dalla, Fabienne Fabre, Lidija Lurakic, Filippo De Luigi, Nando Angelini, Barbara Pilavin, Maria Cumani Quasimodo, Raffaele Triggia, Jose Torres, Fedor Chaliapin, Ferruccio De Ceresa; *distribution:* Cidif; *running time:* 100 minutes; black and white.

Rome, August 1964. The funerals of Palmiro Togliatti, where people turn out en masse, are a traumatic and

crucial passage for more than one generation of Communists. These events provide the emotional climax for four different stories—all emblematic of an identical crisis.

Ermanno, a presumptuous and arrogant young man, has just graduated with a degree in philosophy and doesn't know what to do with his future. Having left his parents and his native Tuscan countryside, he has moved to Rome, where he works as a photographer in the studio of a friend, Muzio. Ermanno boasts his total difference from his family, from his too half-hearted political comrades, and even from Muzio, but he continues to take advantage of all of them. In the end he abandons photography—to which he had previously devoted himself with passion—finding even this insufficient to gratify his ambitions and assuage his anxieties.

Sebastiano, a Bolognese Communist Party official, absolutely must reach Rome with his wife, Giulia, who is suffering from strange obsessions and only after much insistence boards the train. Upon arriving, the couple is met by Paola, a mutual friend who works in Rome. Sebastiano, busy with Party business, leaves his wife in the company of their friend. Circumstances force the two women into each other's constant company, a situation they initially find irksome. In the end, however, they are drawn to each other and discover their homosexuality. Learning of this, Sebastiano is neither able to understand nor, even less, to accept it and makes futile attempts to reconcile with his wife.

Ludovico, a somewhat established film director, is finishing a project about Leonardo da Vinci. He is struck by an illness that at times paralyzes his legs, confining him to long periods of inactivity. The director discovers, along with the protagonist of the film he is shooting, the futility of artistic experience. In fact, his powerful and strong-willed creativity seems to crumble in the wake of an incurable disease revealing all the weaknesses of his character.

Ettore is a young Latin-American revolutionary living in exile in Rome. He expresses himself in radical terms and seems unable to tolerate any sort of tactical approach or uncertainty. But the prospect of his return to Caracas unequivocally arranged by his comrades, makes him waver in his convictions. He confides his fears and doubts to Giovanna, a Roman girl with whom he has a relationship; and she urges him to stay and abandon the struggle. But Ettore, with rancorous pride, rejects this solution and leaves for Nicaragua.

UNDER THE SIGN OF SCORPION (Sotto il segno dello scorpione, 1969)

production: Giuliani G. De Negri for Ager Film; *direction:* Paolo and Vittorio Taviani; *treatment and screenplay:* Paolo e Vittorio Taviani; *photography:* Giuseppe Pinori; *set design:* Gianni Sbarra; *costumes:* Lina Nerli Taviani; *editing:* Roberto Perpignani; *music:* Vittorio Gelmetti; *actors:* Gian Maria Volonté, Lucia Bosè, Giulio Brogi, Samy Pavel,

Subversives.
The actor Giulio Brogi is Ettore, a Latin-American revolutionary exiled in Rome, diverted by discussions in restaurants and sex.

Daniele Rubino, Steffen Zacharias; *distribution:* Cidif; *running time:* 100 minutes; color.

The action unfolds in a mythical time, in an undefined primitive era.

Having survived a terrible volcanic earthquake that has destroyed the island on which they live, a group of men belonging to the Scorpion clan land on an island very similar to their own. They soon learn that, led by Renno, the population of farmers that inhabit it live with the threat of the volcano and attempt to monitor its changes and predict its eruptions.

The shipwreck survivors, guided by Taleno and Rutolo, are determined to escape the capricious tyranny of the volcano once and for all. They have decided to get to the mainland and to establish a new village there. However, the achievement of this plan requires Renno and his people, since they have no possibility of succeeding alone—and above all without women. Initially they try to persuade the island population, recounting the tragic fate of their countrymen and trying to frighten the island inhabitants with the tale of the eruption that destroyed their community. To convince even the most skeptical, Rutolo and his comrades go as far as to act out, the entire dramatic story of the volcanic eruption through an obsessive tribal dance.

The idea of departure begins to spread among the island inhabitants, particularly among the young people. At this point Renno—who hovers between desire to remain and the need to leave—curbs the impetuosity of the new arrivals by having them cast into a pit. Prevented from leaving, the Scorpionites are mocked and humiliated and even subjected to a macabre audio-staging of an volcanic eruption until Renno, who is assailed by constant doubts, allows the Scorpionites to leave, alone, using the community's boats. This will prove to be a fatal error as, once they are free, Rutolo and his men kill the male islanders and abduct all the women.

The Scorpionites finally succeed in reaching the mainland, but the countryside that welcomes them is anything but a garden. Arduous work awaits, punctuated by continuous difficulties: from conflict with the women—who attempt mass suicide to escape their fate—to clashes between the various social groups, and to the harsh conditioning imposed by a newly unyielding form of nature.

ST. MICHAEL HAD A ROOSTER (San Michele aveva un gallo, 1971)

production: Giuliani G. De Negri for Ager Film / RAI TV; *direction:* Paolo and Vittorio Taviani; *treatment and screenplay:* Paolo and Vittorio Taviani, loosely adapted from Leo Tolstoy's *Divine and Human; photography:* Mario Masini; *set design:* Gianni Sbarra; *costumi:* Lina Nerli Taviani; *editing:* Roberto Perpignani; *music:* Benedetto

Under the Sign of Scorpion. **A member of the Scorpion clan on the shore of the Uccellina park, in Tuscany.**

The actress Lucia Bosé with the man of Scorpion clan who abducted her. Now he is in love with her.

Ghiglia; *actors:* Giulio Brogi, Daniele Dublino, Renato Castié, Vito Cipolla, Virginia Ciuffini; *distribution:* Seac; *running time:* 90 minutes; color.

The story, inspired by Tolstoy's *Divine and Human*, takes place around 1870. A band of internationalist anarchists tries to take over a small town in the heart of the Umbrian countryside. The indifference of the inhabitants and the intervention of the army thwarts the effort and leads to the capture of the head of the group, Giulio Manieri. A former mathematics graduate, he comes from a well-to-do family and, having embraced the internationalist faith, earns his living as an ice-cream vendor. Condemned to death, Giulio prepares himself for a martyr's end but, at the last moment, a royal decree stops the firing squad. After the macabre ritual of the cancelled execution that is changed to a life sentence in prison, Giulio is transferred to solitary confinement.

Even in total darkness and solitude, Giulio doesn't want to give in and, in order to keep his mind lucid and his body active, he adopts a regime of rigid discipline: exercise every morning and then mathematics, physics, geometry. His imagination allows him to survive, transforming his rations into delicious meals and populating his cell with comrades, whom Giulio invites to a permanent political reunion. Thus ten years pass, when a decision is made to transfer him to another prison, in the Venetian lagoon.

During the voyage, Giulio's boat draws alongside another, similar one, transporting some young political prisoners to the same destination. Giulio attempts to talk to the group, but he soon realizes that he has nothing in common with the new generation of revolutionaries. The peasant struggles are now anachronistic and propaganda now deals with the working class. Giulio, understanding

that he is utterly excluded from the new phase of struggle, commits suicide by throwing himself into the lagoon.

ALLONSANFAN (1974)

production: Giuliani G. De Negri, for "Una cooperativa cinematografica"; *direction:* Paolo and Vittorio Taviani; *treatment and screenplay:* Paolo and Vittorio Taviani; *photography:* Giuseppe Ruzzolini; *set design:* Giovanni Sbarra; *costumes:* Lina Nerli Taviani; *editing:* Roberto Perpignani; *music:* Ennio Morricone; *actors:* Marcello Mastroianni, Lea Massari, Mimsy Farmer, Laura Betti, Claudio Cassinelli, Benjamin Lev, Bruno Cirino; *running time:* 111 minutes; *distribution:* Italnoleggio; color.

In the years of the Restoration, Fulvio Imbriani, a Lombard aristocrat member of the secret society was suddenly set free from prison. In the attempt of coming out the other associates, the police stated that he was a spy for having revealed the hide-out of their leader Filippo. The brethern were caught in the snare: they accused Fulvio of Filippo's disappearance and went so far as to lynch him. As a matter of fact, the Grand Master committed suicide and the brethern, becoming aware of their mistake, asked Fulvio to forgive them. Since now on, the relationship with his fellows began to crack and Fulvio, ill and weary, disguised himself as a monk and returned to his paternal home, a magnificent villa left twenty years early. He soon revealed his real identity and, thanks to the cares and love of his relatives, he quickly recovered and began to long for a different way of life, far from conflicts and secrecy.

The sudden arrival of his woman Charlotte, who was animated with a firm revolutionary faith, brought him again to reality. Although his feelings to her were

St. Michael had a Rooster. The crossing of a colorless and spectral lagoon.

Rigth: The young revolutionary.

Allonsanfan. Fulvio Imbriani (Marcello Mastroianni) with his son, after the death of his wife Charlotte.

changed, Fulvio asked Charlotte to run away, to take again their son—since his birth entrusted with a family of peasant—and to start a new life. She refused the proposal with disdain and announced the sudden arrival of their comrade. More and more doubtful, Fulvio did not prevent his sister to report them to the police and to lay an ambush; but, in the end, he decided to flee with Charlotte, which was injured during the fight. She did not survive: Fulvio thought to be finally free but he was reached again by the brethren. Joined also by Filippo's son, the young Allonsanfan, they still believed in him and entrusted him with the money of the sect, necessary to buy weapons for an expedition to the South.

Determined to give up with the battle, Fulvio used the money for himself and for his son Massimiliano, with whom wanted to leave towards America. Reached once again, he lied about the arms and cynically caused the death of his comrade Lionello. In the end, he seduced Francesca, Lionello's woman, and persuaded her to be his accomplice in the last snare that he decided to lay to his brethren. In fact, Fulvio wanted to give them to understand that he had recovered the arms; convinced that they could count on the new weapons, the brethren would have left for the South, running into certain death. To give credit to this version, he asked to the girl to wound his leg. Everything was proceeding according to the plan but, becoming delirious for the high temperature, Fulvio invoked the name of Charlotte. Blinded by jealousy,

Francesca decided to revenge herself and, since Fulvio was unconscious, make him embark on the ship going to the South. Later on he woke up and revealed to the comrade the real story about the arms, but it was too late to go back since the ship was already in the open sea.

Soon after the landing, Fulvio carried out the last betrayal. He realised that Vanni, the man who was asked to lead them in those unknown lands, was a dangerous killer. He reported Vanni and his brethren to the police but, just before the arrival of the soldiers, all of them were massacred by the peasants. Only Allonsanfan saved himself but he was so shocked that related to Fulvio of an unreal victory. This one, believing the boy, put on again the red shirt: suddenly he was identified as a revolutionary and killed by the weapons of the army.

PADRE PADRONE (1977)

production: Giuliani G. De Negri for Cinema s.r.l.; *direction:* Paolo and Vittorio Taviani; *treatment and screenplay:* Paolo and Vittorio Taviani, loosely adapted from the homonymous novel by Gavino Ledda; *photography:* Mario Masini; *set design:* Gianni Sbarra; *costumi:* Lina Nerli Taviani; *editing:* Roberto Perpignani; *music:* Egisto Macchi; *actors:* Omero Antonutti, Saverio Marconi, Marcella Michelangeli, Fabrizio Forte, Stanko Molnar, Marino Cenna, Nanni Moretti, Gavino Ledda; *distribution:* Italnoleggio; *running time:* 117 minutes; color.

Padre padrone.
One of the rare
friendly gestures of
the tyrannical father.

Gavino returned to
the village, but his
father doesn't want
to recognise him.

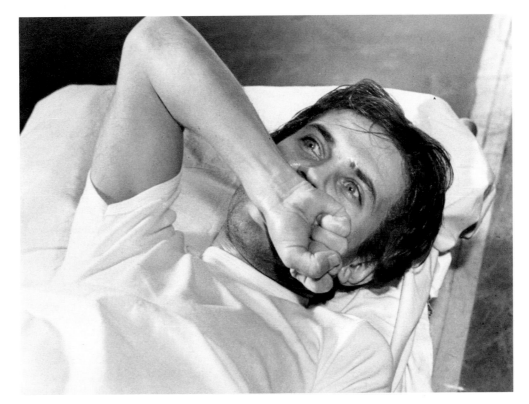

The Meadow.
Giovanni is dying.

Eugenia (Isabella Rossellini) and the children she want to involve in the theatrical activity.

The film is loosely adapted from Gavino Ledda's autobiographical novel, and it is the writer himself who begins and ends the tale. The young Gavino's story begins in Sardinia, in a schoolroom, when his father, the shepherd Efisio—ignoring the requirement for compulsory elementary school education—takes his son and puts him to work in the sheepfold. "The only thing that is truly compulsory," Efisio says, "is poverty," and Gavino, the eldest of his children, must look after the sheep. Once the boy leaves school, nature becomes his alphabet; an alphabet made up of sounds and noises, precise rules and tasks, taught and brutally imposed by his father. Gavino reaches the age of twenty living almost like an animal, in the isolation of the sheepfold until two passing musicians give him an old accordion with which he learns a new language, that of music.

Not even the unexpected legacy of an olive grove delivers Gavino from his fate. A frost destroys all the plants, leading the Ledda family to new and bleaker misery. The boy then decides, along with his other compatriots, to emigrate to Germany, but at the last moment his father's refusal to grant him permission makes his departure impossible. Only some time later, while fulfilling his military service, will Gavino succeed in leaving Sardinia. Reaching the mainland, the first difficulty he encounters is language; he only knows Sardinian dialect. With the help of Cesare, a fellow soldier, he learns to speak Italian and then to read and write. Cesare, who has a college degree, teaches him the basic rudiments of Latin; for Gavino, the language of Virgil becomes an exceptional tool, and he who is utterly closed off, is able to establish a profound friendship with his fellow soldier. With the latter's help, Gavino passes the final exams for school and decides to not pursue a career in the military, as his father had ordained, but to continue his studies, enrolling in the school of Arts and Humanities.

Returning to his family home, he resumes his old habits. Efisio forces him to do harsh work in the fields, preventing him from giving time to his studies. This time, however, Gavino rebels and returns to the mainland where he completes his studies, graduating in linguistics with a thesis on Sardinian dialects.

The film closes, as it begins, with the real Gavino Ledda, having returned to his native land and finally decided to stay there, but with other aspirations and playing a new role.

THE MEADOW (Il prato, 1979)

production: Giuliani G. De Negri for Filmtre; *direction:* Paolo and Vittorio Taviani; *treatment and screenplay:* Paolo and Vittorio Taviani; *photography:* Franco Di Giacomo; *set design:* Gianni Sbarra; *costumes:* Lina Nerli Taviani, Renato Ventura; *editing:* Roberto Perpignani; *music:* Ennio Morricone; *actors:* Isabella Rossellini, Michele Placido, Saverio Marconi, Giulio Brogi, Angela Goodwin,

Remo Remotti, Ermanno Taviani; *distribution:* Cidif; *running time:* 115 minutes; color.

Giovanni, who has just passed a civil service exam and been posted to Milan, cultivates an impossible dream—to make movies. His father, Sergio, a biologist with progressive ideas, asks him to go to San Gimignano to oversee the sale of a family house. This trip, as Giovanni writes to his friend, Leonardo, represents a true turning point in his life. In the small Tuscan town he discovers the fullness of nature in all its suggestiveness and the atavistic, peaceful, and mysterious rhythms of country life. San Gimignano also provides the opportunity for his meeting with Eugenia, a young office worker who manages to cultivate his passion for experimental theater, running a permanent laboratory for the town children.

Giovanni and Eugenia fall in love, but their relationship immediately becomes troubled. In fact the girl is bound to Enzo, a young man who has just graduated with a degree in agriculture, who arrives in San Gimignano to establish an agricultural commune. Despite everything, the two men form a bond of reciprocal respect and even affection. The idea of an open and non-exclusive relationship, encouraged by Enzo and Eugenia, soon comes up against the reality of bitter jealousy, punctuated by thorny contradictions. During an unexpected evacuation of the piazza, where they are putting on one of Eugenia's performances, she falls and hits her head. To avert the danger of a concussion, Enzo and Giovanni, finally united, work together to keep her awake throughout an entire night. But this brief and authentic closeness cannot last and the following day Giovanni leaves San Gimignano.

Having arrived in Milan, the young magistrate leads a monotonous and dissatisfying life. Depressed by a job that seems more absurd every day, he decides—following the logic of self-denial—to request a transfer without prospects to an anonymous court in Puglia. Sergio, his father, is worried about him and offers him all his savings so he can finally make movies, but Giovanni turns him down.

Moving south, Giovanni stops at San Gimignano, just in time to see Eugenia and Enzo who are about to move to Algeria. As the two are leaving, the rabid puppy that Eugenia has given Giovanni, bites him. He contracts the disease and decides to let himself die, asking his father to respect his wishes. Sergio does not comply and calls a helicopter to urgently transport him to a specialized hospital but Giovanni dies immediately after the helicopter takes off from San Gimignano.

THE NIGHT OF THE SHOOTING STARS (La notte di San Lorenzo, 1982)

production: Giuliani G. De Negri for RAI Radiotelevisione Italiana / Ager Cinematografica; *direction:* Paolo and

The Night of the Shooting Stars. The terror of the bombing in a street of San Miniato.

Some people spy on German soldiers from a typical Tuscan hay-loft.

Galvano and his fellows meet the "madman of the eggs".

The encounter with the American soldiers.

Vittorio Taviani; *treatment:* Paolo and Vittorio Taviani; *screenplay:* Paolo and Vittorio Taviani, Giuliani G. De Negri, in collaboration with Tonino Guerra; *photography:* Franco Di Giacomo; *set design:* Gianni Sbarra; *costumes:* Lina Nerli Taviani; *editing:* Roberto Perpignani; *music:* Nicola Piovani; *actors:* Omero Antonutti, Margarita Lozano, Claudio Bigagli, Massimo Bonetti, Norma Martelli, Enrica Maria Modugno, Sabina Vannucchi, Dario Cantarelli, Sergio Dagliana, Giuseppe Furia, Paolo Hendel, Laura Mannucchi, Rinaldo Mirannalti, Miria Guidelli, Micol Guidelli, Giovanni Guidelli, Giorgio Naddi, Renata Zamengo, Massimo Sarchielli, Donata Piacentini, Franco Piacentini, Antonio Prester, David Riondino, Gianfranco Salemi, Massimo Sarchielli, Mario Spallino; *distribution:* Sacis; *running time:* 106 minutes; color.

It is the night of San Lorenzo and, while watching the shooting stars, a young mother tells her little boy about a similar night, many years before, when it was wartime and she, Cecilia, was only six years old. The Germans, who still occupied her town, San Martino, were being closely pursued by the American troops and preparing to withdraw. In the small Tuscan town the Nazis marked many houses with a green cross; before fleeing they would blow them up.

The people awaited the arrival of the allies with trepidation and fear. The Germans had ordered all the inhabitants into the cathedral, assuring the bishop that they would be safe, but that whoever was found elsewhere after sunset would be killed. But fear of the explosion, set for three o'clock in the morning, and the guarantee obtained by the bishop convinced only a few people.

Galvano, a charismatic old farmer, feared reprisals, for the day before a German soldier had been killed behind one of the town walls. Not trusting the Germans' promise, he lead a large group of people through the countryside, in search of the Americans. Dressed in their darkest clothing, Cecilia and her mother also followed Galvano in the desperate march toward safety. Various and diverse destinies are interwoven among the fugitives: Mara, a young Sicilian maid, and Concetta, an elderly well-to-do lady; a young newly married couple, Corrado and Bellindia, and many others.

The young girl experiences the dramatic events of that night of San Lorenzo as a fabulous adventure, punctuated, during moments of authentic terror, by the comforting nursery rhyme taught to her by her mother. During the march some die at the hands of the Fascists but Cecilia survives a clash between the peasants and the Black Shirts, fought in a wheat field, which she transforms into a mythical tale, with the lances, shields and helmets of Achilles and other heroes.

The old peasant was prescient, in fact, after a few

hours, a German mine explodes in the cathedral sowing death and destruction, but most of the group guided by Galvano manages to reach safety. After passing the night in the nearby town of Sant'Angelo, in the morning they hear the chiming church bells of the towns liberated by the Americans. San Martino is among them.

KAOS (1984)

production: Giuliani G. De Negri for RAI Radiotelevisione Italiana and Ager Cinematografica; *direction:* Paolo and Vittorio Taviani; *screenplay:* Paolo and Vittorio Taviani, in collaboration with Tonino Guerra, loosely adapted from Luigi Pirandello's *Short Stories for a Year; photography:* Giuseppe Lanci; *set design:* Francesco Bronzi; *costumes:* Lina Nerli Taviani; *editing:* Roberto Perpignani; *music:* Nicola Piovani; *actors:* Margarita Lozano, Claudio Bigagli, Massimo Bonetti, Enrica Maria Modugno, Anna Malvica, Franco Franchi, Ciccio Ingrassia, Salvatore Rossi, Franco Scaldati, Biagio Barone, Laura Monica, Pasquale Spadola, Omero Antonutti, Regina Bianchi, Laura De Marchi; *distribution:* Dac; *running time:* 188 minutes (television version); 140 minutes (film version); color.

The film, loosely adapted from Pirandello's *Short Stories for a Year,* consists of four tales, a prologue, and an epilogue. In the prologue, some shepherds capture a crow and; at the height of a sadistic game, before freeing it, they tie a bell to its neck. The crow's flight and the sound of the bell tie the different episodes together, from the mountains to the sea of Sicily.

The first episode, *The Other Son,* tells the story of a poor, elderly woman, Maria Grazia, who tries to get in touch with two sons who have emigrated to America, and from whom she has heard no news for fourteen years. The woman gives up hope but, meanwhile, a third son who is nearby, and whom she has resolutely rejected, follows her with solicitude and discretion. His name is Rocco, and he was born of a rape many years earlier. When Garibaldi disembarked on the island, the prisons were opened and bandits freed along with others. Among them was the terrible Comizzi who, after having killed Maria Grazia's husband, abducted and raped her. Rocco's only fault is that he is the spitting image of his father.

The protagonists of the second episode, *Moon Blindness,* are Batà and Sidora, husband and wife for less than a month. One night when the moon is full, Batà orders his wife to lock her in the house and not to open the door for any reason. The man is affected by a form of lycanthropy that leads to terrible attacks of violence. After a night of terror, Sidora takes refuge with her mother who proposes a solution to protect her: that she and Saro, a cousin with whom Sidora was in love, will spend the nights of the full moon with her. For the two cousins, this

Kaos.
The young doctor consoles the neglected mother.
Sidora, frightened by the shrill cries of her husband.
The mother, firm in her grief and rejection of the damned son.

Good Morning Babylon.
The wedding of
Bonanno's sons on
the set of *Intolerance.*

The interventionist
demonstration during
the première
of *Intolerance.*

presents an unexpected occasion to consummate their love. During the first full moon, Saro and Sidora are finally left alone, but the man is tormented by Batà's cries and cannot resist to the urge to go and help him. Embittered at first, it is Sidora who finally goes to assist and rescue her husband.

The third episode, *The Jar*, tells the story of Don Lollò, a wealthy landowner who, to cope with an exceptional olive harvest, acquires an enormous jar. One morning, finding it broken, he calls Zì Dima who is famous for his powerful adhesive. Don Lollò, however, also demands that metal staples also be placed inside the jar. Once the job is done, the workman discovers that he cannot fit through the mouth of the jar thus initiating a harsh standoff between Zì Dima and Don Lollò who is determined not to break his precious container. In the end the wisdom of the astute artisan prevails over the narrow-minded avarice of the old landowner.

The fourth episode, *Requiem*, tells the story of a group of shepherds who live on a large estate where the landowner does not allow them to build a burial ground but forces them to bury their dead in the city, over a day's walk away. The stubbornness of the elderly village head, who goes so far as to feign death and stage his own funeral, gets the better of the landlord's law.

The epilogue, *Conversation with my Mother*, has Pirandello as the protagonist. The writer, at the height of his success, returns to Girgenti after the death of his mother. Arriving at the old family home, he sees the materialized figure of the elderly matriarch who, grasping her son's bitterness, encourages and comforts him with a story he had heard repeatedly in the past. The mother's story transfigures a trip to Malta she took as a child, many years before, into an utterly mythical image, where narration and memory merge.

GOOD MORNING BABYLON (Good Morning Babilonia, 1987)

production: Giuliani G. De Negri for RAI Radiotelevisione Italiana / Filmtre; *direction*: Paolo and Vittorio Taviani; *screenplay*: Paolo and Vittorio Taviani, in collaboration with Tonino Guerra; *photography*: Giuseppe Lanci; *set design*: Gianni Sbarra; *costumes*: Lina Nerli Taviani; *editing*: Roberto Perpignani; *music*: Nicola Piovani; *actors*: Omero Antonutti, Vincent Spano, Joaquim De Almeida, Greta Scacchi, Désirée Becker, Charles Dance, David Brandon, Bérangère Bonvoisin; *distribution*: Istituto Luce / Italnoleggio Cinematografico; *running time*: 118 minutes; color.

The setting is Pisa in the early twentieth century. Master Bonanno and his workers, modern descendants of Medieval artists, have just finished restoring the façade of the cathedral. Despite the unquestionable quality of their work and the talent of the master builder's two sons,

Andrea and Nicola, there is an air of crisis; indeed, having gathered all his men, the elderly Bonanno announces the closing of his business. Given the news, Andrea and Nicola decide to try to make their fortune in America, followed by their father's admonition to "always be equal in every way," because it is precisely in this balance that their power resides.

Arriving in New York, the two brothers find themselves living under the difficult circumstances of immigrants. They know no English and come up against mistrust and prejudice. Two extremely skilled artisans like Andrea and Nicola are offered only jobs at the lowest level, bitter and disillusioned, they end up tending pigs in the middle of the desert. They decide to continue looking and, jumping aboard a train, go first to San Francisco and eventually to Hollywood, to try to find work in the film industry. At first they manage to find only low-level work as laborers, but their ambition pushes them higher. Inspired by the sculpture of Romanesque churches, Andrea and Nicola create the prototype for a large rampant elephant, which they want to present to Griffith for the set of his next film. Despite the harsh opposition of an overbearing producer, who sets the baby elephant afire, Griffith is won over by the Bonanno brothers' idea and hires them to do the set for the Babylon episode of *Intolerance*. Fortune seems to smile upon Andrea and Nicola who, having fallen in love with two young actresses, marry right on the set in the presence of Griffith and, most importantly, of Master Bonanno, who has come to Hollywood for his sons' marriage.

But the brothers' equilibrium is shattered tragically when Edna, Nicola's wife, dies in childbirth. Nicola, mad with desperation, returns to Italy without even seeing his son.

Two years later, during the First World War, Nicola and Andrea meet again in Europe, on the battlefield. About to die, once again "equal in every way," the two brothers film each other with a movie camera so that their sons will have an image to remember them by. In the background, one can make out the façade of a Romanesque church.

NIGHT SUN (Il sole anche di notte, 1990)

production: Giuliani G. De Negri for Filmtre, with the collaboration of Raiuno-Radiotelevisione italiana / Capoul, Intepool, Sara Film di Parigi / Direkt Film of Munich; *direction*: Paolo and Vittorio Taviani; *treatment*: Paolo and Vittorio Taviani, loosely adapted from the story *Father Sergius* by Leo Tolstoy; *screenplay*: Paolo and Vittorio Taviani, in collaboration with Tonino Guerra; *photography*: Giuseppe Lanci; *set design*: Gianni Sbarra; *costumes*: Lina Nerli Taviani; *editing*: Roberto Perpignani; *music*: Nicola Piovani; *actors*: Julian Sands, Charlotte Gainsbourg, Nastassja Kinski, Massimo Bonetti, Margarita Lozano, Patricia Millardet, Rüdiger Vogler, Pamela Villoresi, Geppy

Gleijeses, Sonia Gessner; *distribution:* Sacis (Roma), Bac Films (Francia); *running time:* 113 minutes; color.

The film, loosely adapted from Tolstoy's story *Father Sergius*, is about the baron Sergio Giuramondo who, as a member of the lesser southern nobility, ends up excelling as one of the king's cadets. In fact, Charles III de Bourbon chooses him as his aid-de-camp and offers him the hand of the young Cristina, a duchess of high lineage. For Sergio, the marriage is rather convenient and initially he shows interest. Later, realizing that he is in love, he confides in his betrothed, asking her to forgive his lowly background. Cristina is equally sincere, confessing to the cadet that she has been the king's lover, and this is the only reason her family has decided to agree to their marriage.

His pride wounded, Sergio leaves Cristina's house and the enviable career offered him by King Charles. He returns to his hometown and seeks refuge in the places of his childhood, where he succeeds in overcoming his grief and decides to take religious vows.

The story of Sergio, a cadet in the process of becoming a priest, is known to everyone and he is transformed into an object of exhibition. Disillusioned by the worldly mechanisms of the Church, Father Sergio makes an even more radical choice and withdraws to Mount Petra to lead the life of a hermit, but his fame continues to follow him. Aurelia, a courtesan bored with luxury and comforts, wagers that she can seduce the priest but, instead, Father Sergio—who cuts off a finger in order to resist temptation—achieves his first miracle with her. Struck by his extreme gesture, Aurelia abandons her dissolute life and becomes a nun.

Word of the hermit's supposed miracles spread far and wide and soon the dilapidated and lowly house where he lives, rebuilt by willing churchmen, is assaulted by numerous groups of pilgrims. Among them is Matilda, the very young daughter of a merchant who, since the death of her mother, has been suffering from a strange phobia of sunlight. Weakened by frequent fasts and bitterly saddened by his unwanted notoriety, Father Sergio lets himself be seduced by the girl. When he realizes what he has done, he flees in desperation toward the mountains and, after attempting suicide by throwing himself into a lake; he decides to return to his hometown once again.

When he arrives, he goes in search of an elderly couple, to whom he was very attached, only to discover that the two old people have died. The miracle they had requested from him has come true: the two died together, as they desired. But the hermit has also received a blessing: the peasants whom he has just met don't recognize him but have taken pity and offered aid. Finally free from his fame and pride, Father Sergio begins an anonymous new life, among the most humble of people and, from that moment, all trace of him is lost.

Sergio asks forgiveness to the girl who seduced him.

Previous page, from the top: Margarita Lozano treats the injured foot of young Sergio.

Waiting for the procession in the streets of Naples.

Father Sergio works in the country trying to purify himself from the worldly vanities.

FIORILE (1993)

production: Grazia Volpi for Filmtre / Gierre Film, with the collaboration of Penta Film; *direction:* Paolo and Vittorio Taviani; *screenplay:* Sandro Petraglia, Paolo and Vittorio Taviani; *photography:* Giuseppe Lanci; *set design:* Gianni Sbarra; *costumes:* Lina Nerli Taviani; *editing:* Roberto Perpignani; *music:* Nicola Piovani; *actors:* Claudio Bigagli, Galatea Ranzi, Michael Vartan, Lino Capolicchio, Athina Cenci, Norma Martelli, Pier Paolo Capponi, Chiara Caselli, Renato Carpentieri, Costanze Engelbrecht; *distribution:* Italnoleggio; *running time:* 118 minutes; color.

Originally from Tuscany, Luigi Benedetti has lived in Paris for many years with his wife and children, Simona and

Emilio. When his father unexpectedly has a heart attack, he decides to return to Tuscany with his entire family to convince him to move with them to Paris. Father and son have not seen each other for ten years, and the two children have never known their grandfather. Traveling by car over the Tuscan roads, Luigi tells his children the tormented story, half-legend, half-reality, of the Benedetti family. In that setting, the characters evoked by Luigi become real, making the words of his story come alive.

The story, tied to an ancient curse, begins at the time of the Napoleonic campaigns. Along their march into Italy, the French troops were frequently attacked by haggard and disorganized groups of nobles. During one of these assaults Jean, a young French lieutenant charged with guarding the regiment strongbox, hides in the woods. There he meets a girl, Elisabetta, and it is love at first sight. With her, he forgets the battle and leaves the box of gold unguarded. Corrado Benedetti, the girl's brother, comes upon the gold and claims it and, for failing in his duty, the lieutenant is condemned to death by his comrades. Jean, thinking of Elisabetta, completely unaware that she cannot save him, writes her last love letter, naming it Fiorile, after the eighth month of the new French calendar—the springtime and the revolutionary ideals.

The gold taken from Jean brings the Benedetti family enormous wealth and a terrible curse, and a century later their descendents will pay the price. Alessandro Benedetti, to safeguard his political career, wants to separate his sister Elisa from the young farmer she loves. The latter is forced to emigrate to Buenos Aires and has the girl believe she has been betrayed and abandoned. Despite Alessandro's machinations, Elisa is expecting a child and is determined to have an abortion until she discovers the deception and decides to carry her pregnancy to term and to poison her brothers.

The curse of the gold continues to strike the Benedetti family and, one generation later, it is Massimo, Elisa's nephew, who pays the price. As a child, teased by his playmates, he had taken refuge in music, comforted by the spirit of Jean, his good and pure ancestor. A young student of literature, still obsessed with the name he bears, Massimo and his girlfriend Chiara become involved in the Resistance, viewing his experience with the partisan struggle as the upholding of Jean's ideals. Captured by the Fascists, he is inspired by his ancestor and writes a letter to Chiara as he awaits the firing squad. Shortly before being shot, recognized as a Benedetti, Massimo is saved. The hatred of the people and news of the death of his beloved cast him into profound grief. Exchanging suffering for madness, he goes to live in a clinic for some time. Later, fearful of the curse, he sells off all his property at a loss and distances himself from Luigi, the child he had with Chiara, by having him raised elsewhere. This is the same Luigi who is now telling the story of the Benedetti.

Fiorile. **A grieved and deceptive mother.**

Fraternal love and deceptions in the elegant interiors of Villa La Petraia.

Luigi's story ends here, at the threshold of the home of his father, Massimo. However, the curse, which finally seemed defeated by the serene rationality of the new nuclear family, is embedded in Simona and Emilio, who are profoundly struck by their father's words and by the mysterious figure of their grandfather. The girl writes the word "Fiorile" on a misted over window, while her brother clenches gold coin in his fist.

ELECTIVE AFFINITIES (Le affinità elettive, 1996)

production: Grazia Volpi for Filmtre / Gierre Film, in collaboration with RAI Radiotelevisione italiana, Florida Movies, France 3, with the participation of Canal Plus; *direction:* Paolo and Vittorio Taviani; *screenplay:* Paolo and Vittorio Taviani, from J. W. Goethe's *Elective Affinities*; *photography:* Giuseppe Lanci; *set design:* Gianni Sbarra; *costumes:* Lina Nerli Taviani; *editing:* Roberto Perpignani; *music:* Carlo Crivelli; *actors:* Isabelle Huppert, Fabrizio Bentivoglio, Jean Hugues Anglade, Marie Gillain, Massimo Popolizio, Laura Marinoni, Stefania Fuggetta; *italiana distribution:* Filmauro (Italy), Sacis (International); *running time:* 120 minutes; color.

The film is a loose adaptation of Goethe's novel and transposes the story of the four lovers to a Tuscan setting.

During a reception at the Medici villa in Poggio a Caiano, the Countess Carlotta and the Baron Edoardo meet after spending many years apart. The two, who loved each other intensely in the past, decide to marry, seizing the possibility of a late but desired happiness. The wedding is celebrated in the church of San Miniato al Monte, beloved by both, though for opposite reasons. Carlotta appreciates the church's decorative geometric rationalism, while Edoardo sees in that same geometry the charm of an archaic mystery.

The couple moves onto the Baron's estate, planning to renovate it according to the most modern scientific developments. A year passes and the couple seems to have found a stable equilibrium. Edoardo, initially coming up against his wife's fears, invites his dearest friend, the architect Ottone, to the villa. Carlotta's fears prove to be well founded, however, as Ottone's presence brings joy and liveliness but disturbs the family *menage*.

One evening, after having read a passage dedicated to the affinities of elements in nature, Carlotta proposes that they ask Ottilia, her adoptive daughter who has been raised at a boarding-school, to come live with them. The law of attraction between elements shifts from the realm of chemistry to that of human relationships: Carlotta and Ottone fall in love, as do Ottilia and Edoardo. The former are rational and controlled, while the other two are passionate; together, the four seem to achieve their natural equilibrium. But at a certain point the affinities

Elective Affinities. **Edoardo, Ottilia and the child, linked by a destiny of death.**

The mourning of Ottilia: she has decided to let herself die.

The four resume their lives in the villa, but nothing is as it was. Ottilia is closed off in absolute silence and, rejecting food, allows herself to die. Upon hearing the news, Edoardo also dies and, finally united, the two lovers are buried together in the villa chapel. Ottone abandons the estate, leaving Carlotta his watch, as a token of the impossibility of his return.

TU RIDI (1998)

production: Grazia Volpi for Filmtre, in collaboration with Dania film and RAI Cinemafiction; *direction:* Paolo and Vittorio Taviani; *treatment and screenplay:* Paolo and Vittorio Taviani, from Luigi Pirandello's *Short Stories for a Year; photography:* Giuseppe Lanci; *set design:* Gianni Sbarra; *costumes:* Lina Nerli Taviani; *editing:* Roberto Perpignani; *music:* Nicola Piovani; *actors:* Antonio Albanese, Giuseppe Cederna, Luca Zingaretti, Dario Cantarelli, Elena Ghiaurov, Sabrina Ferilli, Lello Arena, Turi Ferro, Steve Spedicato, Ludovico Caldarera, Roberto Fuzio, Orio Scaduto; *distribution:* Rai Trade; *running time:* 103 minutes; color.

The film, inspired by Pirandello's short stories, consists of two tales. The first episode unfolds during the Fascist era. The protagonist is Felice, a former successful tenor who, forced by a weak heart to give up singing, works as a book-keeper at a theater. He is married to Marika, a young Rumanian woman whom he met during a tour of Eastern Europe. The relationship between the two has long cooled, and he is happy, or "felice," only in name and at night, when a dream he can never remember makes him break out in irresistible laughter in his sleep, which in turn infuriates his wife. His frustrating office work is lightened by the presence of Tobia, his colleague and friend, to whom he is tied by an affectionate complicity.

One morning upon waking, Felice manages to remember the dream that has given him so much laughter. It is a terrible dream in which the daily humiliation inflicted on Tobia by Gino Migliore, the overbearing head of the theater, is repeated and amplified. Felice, abandoned by Marika and still dazed by his sense of guilt toward Tobia, gets word of his friend's suicide, and decides to follow him, but not before having avenged him. He follows Migliori home to humiliate and frighten him to death with a toy pistol and then goes to the sea, having decided to drown himself. Not even a fortuitous and happy meeting with Nora, a singer he knew during his successful years as a tenor, succeeds in dissuading him.

The second episode, set in the present, tells the story of a kidnapping. Vincenzo, young son of a Mafioso arrested by the police, is abducted upon the orders of an organized Mafia group. Held hostage in order to prevent his father from squealing, the boy becomes friends with Rocco, his jailer. The two are hidden in the mountains near Mount

become extremely strong and irresistible, so that Carlotta and Edoardo make love for an entire night, imagining they are with their respective new loves. A baby is born from that strange night of love, Carlotta and Edoardo's son, but with Ottone's red hair and Ottilia's beauty mark.

The arrival of the newborn causes the couples to break up, the two men move away, leaving Carlotta and Ottilia on the estate to take care of the baby. Ottone, stronger and more rational, is called to Venice for work, to which he devotes himself entirely. Edoardo, incapable of giving up Ottilia, enlists in the army, looking for death in every battle. Gravely wounded, he entrusts himself to the care of his best friend and, after a long convalescence, persuades him to return to the estate to resolve his relationship with the women. Ottone will have to convince Carlotta to consent to a divorce, so that finally the two couples will be able to be reunited, but a terrible tragedy prevents their dreams from coming true: while Ottilia is distracted, the child falls into the lake and drowns.

Ballarò, and live alone in a large abandoned hotel. Vincenzo's kidnapping echoes a story from one hundred years before: that of Doctor Ballarò, an elderly country doctor, abducted by three deprived peasants from the area. The three lead him to an isolated shed but soon realize they cannot obtain any ransom from Ballarò's relatives. While they don't want to kill their hostage, because he has recognized them, they know they cannot set him free so, guarded in shifts, the doctor will spend the rest of his life in that shed. In captivity, the kidnappers become fascinated by the knowledge of the old man who reveals to them the rules of the cosmos, the mysterious force of gravity, and the mobile nature of light. In the end the kidnappers, with their wives and children, become his family and Doctor Ballarò will die in the mountains to which he gave his name, surrounded by the affection of that strange band.

A tragically different end awaits Vincenzo. After his father's change of heart, Rocco kills the boy and dissolves him in a basin of sulfuric acid.

RESURRECTION (Resurrezione, 2001)*

production: Filmtre / Rai (Italy); Pampa Productions / France 2 (France); Bavaria Film (Germany); *direction:* Paolo and Vittorio Taviani; *treatment and screenplay:* Paolo and Vittorio Taviani, from the homonymous Leo Tolstoy's novel; *set design:* Lorenzo Baraldi; *costumes:* Lina Nerli Taviani; *editing:* Roberto Perpignani; *music:* Nicola Piovani; *actors:* Stefania Rocca, Timothy Peach, Maria Baumer, Cecile Bois, Eva Christian, Sonia Gessner, Giulia Lazzarini, Michela Melega, Vania Vilers, Marina Vlady, Antonella Ponziani, Giulio Scarpati; *international distribution:* Rai Trade; *running time:* 188 minutes; color.

It is a story about the anxiety of redemption and expiation that strikes Dimitri Nechliudov—a spoiled and insensitive nobleman, who has abandoned the ideals of his youth—when, as a judge of the people, a prostitute, accused of complicity in a murder, is brought before him. He recognizes her as a girl he was in love with many years before and who, pushed by his "animal spirit," he had seduced and paid off with one hundred rubles. He tries to have her acquitted and, failing in this, he follows her to Siberia and asks her to marry him, although he doesn't love her. She, however, turns him down, precisely because she has come to love him again.

* This entry was written before the final edition of *Resurrection*; differently from the others films, the indications were not taken form the credits, but form the artistic and technical cast given to us be the production. The summary of the plot was reassumed directly from the screenplay.

Tu ridi. **Top: The game before the murder.**
Above: In the shocking ending, the killer's hallucinated dance.

LATEST PUBLICATIONS ON CINEMA:

"Acting is almost better than making love", Mastroianni used to say. Acting was fun. Marcello played more than 130 films during 40 years of exciting cinema. This book is a lavishly illustrated biography (with photos never before seen in the USA!) enriched by cast and credits of all his films. This is the enthralling story of Fellini's favorite actor, unique in his field.

192 pages • US$ 29.95

An homage to the greatest Italian diva of all times. This beautiful and lavishly illustrated volume (with photos never before seen) covers the brilliant career of the esteemed Italian actress. The Authors tell us about the debuts, the fears, the films – enriched by cast and credits – and the world stardom of this beautiful and glamorous woman.

204 pages • US$ 29.95

This volume it is not simply another book on the director of La Dolce Vita, but the definitive screening in words, at the beginning of this century, of the man, the shadow and the magic of the most ingenious Italian innovator of contemporary cinema.

192 pages • US$ 29.95

Germany's '30s-'40s era film stars were appreciated not for their National Socialist virtues, but for their wit, beauty and ability to make Germans forget about their violent present. Tainted Goddesses includes biographies of these women of the Nazi era, such as Zarah Leander, Linda Baarova or Brigitte Horney, along with rare photographs, synopses and credits of their most important films.

182 pages • US$ 19.95

OTHERS GREMESE TITLES ON CINEMA

Claudio G. Fava
ALBERTO SORDI
An American in Rome
190 pages • US$ 39.95

Oreste De Fornari
SERGIO LEONE
The Great Italian Dream
of Legendary America
168 pages • US$ 39.95

Jean A. Gili
ITALIAN FILMAKERS
Self Portraits: a Selection
of Interviews
160 pages • US$ 24.95

Stefano Masi-Enrico Lancia
ITALIAN MOVIE GODDESSES
Over 80 of the Greatest
Women in Italian Cinema
224 pages • US$ 29.95

Stefano Masi
ROBERTO BENIGNI
80 pages • US$ 12.95